How the Military Created Your Phone

How the Military Created Your Phone and Why That Matters

Púca Jinn

Preface

How the Military Created Your Phone and Why That Matters traces the evolution of information technology from the invention of the telegraph to the latest advancements in artificial intelligence. It documents the role the US Department of Defense played in developing these technologies and explains how they propelled the world into the Information Technology Era.

The opinions expressed in this book stem from twenty-five years selling technology to government and defense on behalf of several of the world's largest and most influential high-tech companies. As such, I am solely responsible for any errors or omissions.

"People will come to love their oppression, to adore the technologies that undo their capacities to think."
Aldous Huxley

What hath God Wrought?

The American Civil War ushered in the age of modern warfare. For the first time, mass citizen armies clashed using technologies developed during the Industrial Revolution: the camera documented the battlefield, troops were transported to the front lines in trains; ironclads rendered wooden warships obsolete; rifled barrels replaced smooth-bore firearms; and reconnaissance balloons provided aerial views of the battlefield.

Alone among the technologies used during the Civil War, the telegraph harnessed the revolutionary potential of electricity. Through its dots and dashes, the telegraph signaled the ebb of the Industrial age and the birth of the modern Information Technology Era.[1]

Although several scientists in different countries contributed to the development of the telegraph, American Samuel Morse is chiefly credited with its invention.

---

[1] Sir William Samuel Stephenson, CC, MC, DFC, was a Canadian soldier, airman, businessman, inventor, and lightweight boxing champion. He served as Director of the British Security Coordination (British Secret Intelligence Service) during WWII and is considered the Godfather of the Office of Strategic Services (OSS), the precursor to the CIA. Although he was the first non-American to receive America's highest award for a civilian, the Presidential Medal of Merit, his most prized possession was the worn and polished telegraph key he built and used as a teenager, which occupied a place of honor in the private study of his Bermuda retirement home.

Samuel Finley Morse was born in Boston, Massachusetts, in 1791. A portrait painter by trade, Morse married Lucretia Walker in 1818. Seven years later, Morse was in Washington D.C., painting a portrait of the Marquis de Lafayette, when he received a letter informing him that his wife was seriously ill. Morse hurried home to Connecticut, but before he arrived, Lucretia had passed away and been laid to rest. Grief-stricken and possessing a basic understanding of how electricity functioned, Morse abandoned painting and devoted himself to advancing long-distance communication.

In 1837, Morse filed for a patent for his telegraph machine. Although his original design has been refined, its core mechanics remain unchanged.

Telegraph machines are electromechanical devices that utilize electricity to open and close a physical connection between a transmitter and a receiver. When an operator depresses the telegraph's key, the circuit is closed, and an electrical pulse is transmitted down a wire to the receiver, activating an electromagnet. This electromagnet attracts the metallic armature of the receiver's key, causing it to strike a base plate producing the telegraph's trademark click sound.

Morse's other significant contribution to telegraphy was the code that still bears his name. Developed in collaboration with his colleague Alfred Vail and based on an existing code used by German railways, Morse Code quickly became the standard for international communications.

The Morse system assigned a unique combination of long and short pulses – dashes and dots - to each letter or number, with the simplest code sequences assigned to the most frequently repeated letters. Holding the telegraph key down produced a long pulse or dash. Releasing the key quickly created a short pulse or dot. By stringing these code sequences together to form words, a coded message could be rapidly transmitted over great distances.[2]

Morse's three state encoding system; dot, dash and rest, would remain the universal standard for electronic communications well into the 1960s when it was replaced by our current two state system; binary.

With his prototype telegraph machine and code in hand, Morse was eager to showcase the advantages of his new system. But first, he needed the capital to procure and install two miles of copper cable.[3] After several failed attempts, Morse finally secured the financial backing of Maine congressman Francis Smith. Following a successful trial, Congress appropriated $30,000 to construct an experimental 38-mile telegraph line between Washington, D.C., and Baltimore along the Baltimore and Ohio Railroad. The first telegraph line commenced operations on May 24, 1844, when Morse transmitted his now-famous words: "What hath God wrought?"

Opinions were divided regarding the telegraph's utility. Skeptics scoffed the enormous cost of stringing and maintaining copper cables would exceed revenues. Supporters enthused the telegraph would shrink the world and propel humanity into a new utopian age.

The telegraph's early development mirrored that of the railroads and modern cable companies. Independent lines sprang up between localities, which were, in turn, consolidated into regional conglomerates, with Western Union emerging as the national leader.

---

[2] Morse Code laid the foundation for the encryption technologies used during both World Wars. It was the need to decipher these codes that led to the development of modern computers.

[3] A repeater was necessary to amplify a telegraph signal over distances exceeding two miles.

Eavesdropping on electronic communications began during the Civil War. In the North, Secretary of War Edwin M. Stanton centralized telegraph communications within the War Department, effectively creating the first National Security Agency (NSA). Centralizing all lines permitted Stanton to surveil troves of journalistic, governmental, and personal data. It also enabled Washington officials to monitor the war's progress in real-time, manage logistics, and provide near real-time direction to Union field commanders.

The military necessity for secure messaging forced both sides to develop sophisticated encrypting and decrypting techniques creating a cadre of highly skilled signals officers. When the war ended in 1865, the North had sent over six million messages and strung an additional 15,000 miles of telegraph cable. War also proved profitable for Western Union which exited the conflict with two and a half times its prewar cable infrastructure and a fourfold increase in enterprise value.

***"Mr. Watson, come here; I want you."* - Alexander Graham Bell**

Between the end of the American Civil War in 1865 and the onset of the Great War in 1914, scientists probed the mysteries of electromagnetic waves, and Alexander Graham Bell patented the telephone.

Bell, whose wife and mother were deaf, posited that the mechanics of hearing could be replicated electronically. Understanding that hearing involves sound waves vibrating the eardrum, Bell envisioned a diaphragm capable of converting these waves into electric signals. In 1877, Bell successfully created a prototype based on this principle, and the telephone company that still bears his name was born.

Like most innovations, the telephone was primarily an enhancement of an existing technology, the telegraph - aligning with the principle that technological advancements are primarily evolutionary, not revolutionary. Bell's only real contribution had been the introduction of a diaphragm. Perceiving how closely the two devices were related, he offered to sell his fledgling enterprise to Western Union for $100,000. Fortunately for Bell, whose telephone company proved to be far more profitable, Western Union declined.

One reason for Bell's success was that, unlike the telegraph, which required skilled workers; a restriction which limited its use primarily to government and business, anyone could use a telephone. And since Bell rented rather than sold telephones, most American households could afford one.

However, like Prometheus' gift of fire, the new technology came with a cost. The transition from owner to user had profound implications for privacy rights. The first telephones were located in public places where conversations could be overheard. To remedy this, the telephone company introduced telephone booths. But switchboard operators frequently eavesdropped on calls, and most houses were connected via "party lines," where others could and did listen in.

More relevant to our story, just as the telegraph enabled electronic eavesdropping on military communications, the widespread adoption of the telephone made state-sponsored mass surveillance practicable for the first time. America had entered the Information-Technology Age.

Going Wireless - *"Any Sufficiently Advanced Technology is Indistinguishable from Magic."* - Arthur C. Clarke

In 1885, Heinrich Hertz, a brilliant German physicist employed by the Karlsruhe Institute of Technology, experimentally demonstrated the electromagnetic waves postulated by Scottish physicist James Clerk Maxwell.

Electromagnetic wave technology was economically more viable because it enabled electronic signals to travel long distances without cables. Stringing and maintaining copper cables between every sender and receiver was costly and labor-intensive, hindering widespread adoption. In contrast, radio functions on the principle of one-to-many, just as Wi-Fi operates today.

Military researchers in different countries began experimenting with the new technology, and by the outbreak of war in 1914, all of the major powers possessed crude wireless systems. In the United States, radio was mainly a hobby for enthusiasts. Broadcasting, as we understand it today, did not emerge until after the Great War.

In 1909, Bell sought control of Western Union in a bid to monopolize the United States telecommunications network. When the US Justice Department "expressed its concerns," Bell "voluntarily" divested himself of Western Union shares.

By the turn of the century, every country except the United States had brought telecommunications under state control. The US flirted with this model when it took over the nation's telecommunications as a temporary war measure in 1917 but unwilling to bear the ongoing cost, soon returned it to private interests.

The Airplane – Third Dimensional Warfare

In 1898, the United States War Department awarded $50,000 to Samuel Langley, the Director of the Smithsonian Institution, to design and construct an engine-powered aircraft for military purposes. Despite his best efforts and prodding from the War Department, Langley failed. Five years later, on December 17, 1903, Orville and Wilbur Wright made their first of four successful flights in Kitty Hawk, North Carolina.[4] Unlike Langley, the Wright brothers received no government funding.

To protect their intellectual property, the Wrights kept their work secret and shifted operations to Huffman Prairie, Ohio, to refine their design. Satisfied with their improved model, they secured a patent and contacted the US Army.

In August 1908, Orville delivered a prototype to the parade grounds at Fort Myer, Virginia, near Arlington National Cemetery, for flight trials. Impressed by the Wright design, the Army issued a solicitation based on its specifications. Funding for the procurement was based on the $30,000 price tag Wilbur set during meetings held with the Board of Ordnance and Fortification in late 1907. That same year, the Army stood up an Aeronautical Division staffed by three junior officers to prepare for the acquisition.[5]

The Wright brothers delivered their first airplane to the United States Army Signal Corps on Aug. 2, 1909. Officially designated Signal Corps No. 1, it was commonly called the Wright Military Flyer.

---

[4] Concerned for their safety, their father, Milton, made Orville and Wilbur promise never to fly together.

[5] Lieutenant Selfridge died on September 17, 1908, in a crash during a demonstration flight in a Wright brothers' aircraft, marking the first of many fatalities among early flight training trainees.

Eager for additional sales, the Wrights shipped an airplane to Europe and soon established contracts with the governments of Britain, Germany, and France.

The Great War - *"...a war to end all wars."* Woodrow Wilson

In August 1914, Imperial Germany went to war determined to wage two short one-front battles rather than a long two-front war she could not hope to win. The plan, devised by Field Marshal Alfred von Schlieffen, whose last words were rumored to have been, "keep the right wing very strong," was to knock off the French Army in a lightning sweep through neutral Belgium,[6] around the French left flank, before France's Russian allies could mobilize.

Unfortunately for the Germans, France's prewar loans to Russia had been well spent. An extensive network of westward-facing railroad tracks[7] had been laid, and frontier stations with expanded platforms to accommodate large troop trains were also constructed. Consequently, the Russian Army mobilized much faster than German war planners anticipated.

No one likes to see their plans go awry, especially German General Staffs.[8] So they did what all General Staffs

---

[6] When Germany invaded Belgium on August 4, 1914, at the outset of World War I, they violated the 1839 Treaty of London, which guaranteed Belgium's neutrality. This breach was a crucial factor in Britain's decision to enter the war against Germany, as Britain, a signatory to the treaty, had pledged to defend Belgium's neutrality.

[7] Russian and German railroads employed different track gauges, with the Russian gauge being three inches wider. This design was intended to prevent either side from using the other's tracks in the event of war.

[8] The organization of the German General Staff in 1806 set a precedent for centralized military planning and management, influencing military organization globally and serving as a model for other nations in developing their staff systems. It was later adopted as the executive model for modern corporations.

do: blamed the two officers commanding their eastern army, cashiered them, and replaced them with two others.

The first, Paul von Hindenburg, was a retired career soldier descended from a minor Prussian aristocratic family. Hindenburg would rise to head the German Army, lose the war, and then blame it on Germany's post-war government, which had virtually no say in its conduct. A scant seven years later, he was elected President of the German Republic based on his pledge to avoid war and unite the fragmented nation. Hindenburg's most infamous act during his two terms as Germany's President was to appoint Adolf Hitler - whom he personally despised, as Chancellor in 1933. "That man for a Chancellor?" scoffed Hindenburg, "I'll make him a postmaster, and he can lick stamps with my head on them."

The second, Hindenburg's deputy, Erich Friedrich Wilhelm Ludendorff, was a brilliant staff officer who disdained peace as "an interval between wars." Less astute in post-war politics than Hindenburg, Ludendorff allowed himself to be duped into endorsing Hitler's nascent National Socialist party.

Arriving together by private train on the Eastern front on 23 August 1914, Hindenburg and Ludendorff's first command decision was to approve plans already set in motion by the interim commander, General Carl Adolf Maximilian Hoffmann. Hoffmann intended to bring the Second of two Russian armies to battle before the First could come to their aid. Consequently, there was a great deal of handwringing at German Headquarters regarding the location and movements of the First Russian Army.

Fortunately for Hindenburg and Ludendorff, both First and Second Army lacked an adequate supply of telephone cable. The shortage was primarily due to the Russian Czar, who conceived that suppressing telecommunications technology was the best way to immunize his regime from revolutionary ideas. As a result, Russian commanders had to rely on wireless technologies for inter-army communications. Worse, commander of First Army, the mustachioed General Paul von Rennenkampf, possessed a code book for encrypting and decrypting messages, but General Alexander Samsonov, in command of Second Army - whom Rennenkampf despised, did not. Consequently, Rennenkampf's battle plans were broadcast to First Army command in the clear. Intercepted by astounded German radio operators, the translated communiqué was sped by motorcycle courier to German Command Headquarters.

With Rennenkampf's position and intentions happily in hand, Hindenburg and Ludendorff were free to withdraw troops from Rennenkampf's front and speed them by train to reinforce their attack on Samsonov. As a result, the Russian Second Army was crushed at what became known as the Battle of Tannenberg. Samsonov, disgraced, retreated into a nearby wood and shot himself.

Landline versus Mobile Communications

Despite the crucial role signal intelligence (SIGINT) had played in the Battle of Tannenberg, the Germans did not establish a dedicated unit to systematically monitor enemy radio traffic for a full year. There were two main reasons for this:

First, all belligerents went to war in 1914, equipped primarily with wire-based communications. Reequipping forces with radio-based communication equipment, and training operators to effectively use it, took time.

Second, radio was still in its infancy. Prewar radio sets were too bulky and heavy for trench warfare, requiring as many as ten mounted men and four pack mules to transport them. The soldiers who operated them soon found themselves targets. Early transmitters required tall antennae. Once erected, communication centers were quickly identified by enemy artillery spotters.

Finally, the requirements for encoding and decoding messages, combined with the inherent unreliability and limited range of these early sets, caused them to be regarded – initially at least - as strictly auxiliary to wired systems. This thinking changed as incessant shellfire severed land lines.

In 1917, scientists from the Allied countries developed the super-heterodyne receiver—an innovative way to tune radios and allow them to pick up distant signals. The receiver superimposed one radio wave on top of another, greatly amplifying and filtering the resulting intermediate frequency. This was then demodulated to generate an audio signal, which was in turn amplified for output to loudspeakers—industry-specific jargon that explains why so many technocrats are physicists.

The British Army introduced several hundred continuous-wave wireless sets in the same year. Unlike earlier spark-based sets, that had a very short range: continuous-wave sets had a range of eleven kilometers or more. Eventually, all armies developed smaller and more portable sets powered by storage batteries, which, fortunately for their operators, employed shorter, less conspicuous antennae.

The introduction of airplanes to the battlespace further underscored the need for high-powered portable radios. Communication between flyers and ground commanders was cumbersome and slow during the Great War - pilots had to land or drop messages to provide reports while black and white cloth panels were spread out in open fields to convey surface-to-air commands. Both sides committed substantial resources to improving radiotelegraph and radiotelephone technologies to address these challenges.

As early as 1910, scientists had already demonstrated that wireless transmissions between aircraft and the ground were possible. Trials involved pilots tapping Morse code on a transmitter balanced on their laps. There were, however, a few problems with this method. First, engine noise tended to drown out the sound of incoming messages. Second, airmen were understandably more concerned about being shot down than operating a code key. Clearly, voice radio would be necessary for wireless communication to become practical in the air. But voice transmissions required higher frequencies than Morse code, and early radios were too big and heavy to be carried aloft by the underpowered wood and canvas aircraft of the time.

Spurred on by the exigencies of war, engineers on both sides raced to make necessary improvements. In 1916, the French successfully tested crude air-to-ground voice communication during the battle of Verdun. One year later, they demonstrated air-to-air voice communication at Villacoublay. Transmitters became standard aboard German aircraft in 1916, and receivers also became standard by the end of that same year.

Radio and the War at Sea - Surface Fleets

In 1914, the battleship was the yardstick by which great powers measured military prowess. Besides cutting-edge technologies for propulsion, navigation, communications, and fire control systems, battleships provided their crews with amenities most civilians only dreamt of - electric lights, central heating, hot running water, and flush toilets. They even featured electric galleys and washing machines. Not surprisingly, the construction and maintenance of these technological behemoths was ruinous, straining British and German prewar national budgets to their breaking points.[9]

With so much treasure and, in Britain's case, national security at stake[10], both sides kept tight reins on their sea-going admirals. Indeed, as Winston Churchill pointed out, Admiral of the British Fleet, Sir John Jellicoe, was "the only man on either side who could lose the war in an afternoon." It was fortunate for the politicians, therefore – but not the harangued admirals - that high-powered shore stations made wireless communication over long distances possible. Practically every move that British, French, or German admirals made during the war was the result of a radio order from their respective War Office. England directed the maneuvers of her fleets from the Marconi station at Carnarvon in Wales, Germany from Nauen, and France from Paris.

But as at Tannenberg, the use of radio to control naval operations proved a two-edged sword. Prior to the German Cruiser Emden's destruction of a radio station on Direction Island off the coast of Western Australia on November 9, 1914, one of Direction's operators tapped out an SOS. The HMS Sydney intercepted the transmission, and the Emden was sunk in a follow on engagement. In 1915, in East Africa, a Curtis seaplane transmitted a location fix for the German cruiser Königsberg to a nearby Royal Navy squadron, which

---

[9] In the lead-up to World War I, Britain's and Germany's relentless spending on naval armaments placed enormous strain on their national treasuries. The financial burden grew so severe that it triggered widespread public outcry in Britain and fears of imminent bankruptcy.

[1010] The creation of its "luxury fleet" had always been more about the Kaiser's ego than Germany's security.

caught and sank her. The SMS Dresden was also located based on intercepted wireless messages, and it was intercepted wireless traffic that alerted the British Navy to the movements of the German High Seas Fleet, leading to the only major naval battles of the Great War: the Battle of Dogger Bank in January 1915 and the Battle of Jutland in May 1916.

Room 40

The British Admiralty also had far more effective methods of surveilling German fleet movements at their disposal. In the old Admiralty building, down the corridor from the First Sea Lord's office, there was a small room known simply as Room 40.[11] Within this inconspicuous office, a small band of Naval Intelligence officers, German scholars, and university dons used captured enemy code books to decipher German Navy wireless messages.

Once deciphered, the decrypts were sealed in a red envelope[12] and sent by messenger to a senior intelligence officer, who personally delivered the most critical messages to the First Lord, First Sea Lord, and the Admiralty War Group. From there, the information, though not its source, was disseminated to those with "a need to know."

As the war dragged on and the sudden appearance of British ships could no longer be ascribed to coincidence, the German High Seas Fleet commander-in-chief began looking for explanations. Spies, traitors, and the monitoring of German ship movements by neutral fishing trawlers were all

---

[11] The Royal Navy had strong connections to the secret service because, unlike the British Army, its officers frequently traveled to foreign countries on naval assignments. Consequently, James Bond is depicted as a Commander in the British Navy.

[12] Giving way later to a locked red box.

suspected but the German Navy never guessed the British had broken their codes.

By the time the Great War ended on November 11, 1918, room 40 had decoded 20,000 German wireless messages.

War on the U-Boats

In 1914, the British strategy for war at sea was twofold: blockade Germany's ports, choking off the flow of imports that fueled her domestic economy and war machine, and keep Germany's High Seas Fleet from breaking out into the Atlantic, where she could attack Allied merchant shipping. Since the Germans did not believe their High Seas Fleet could defeat the British Navy in a sustained naval battle - calculus the Battle of Jutland proved correct; the Germans built undersea boats (U-boats) to evade Britain's fleet and harry her merchant shipping.

During WWI, U-boat technology was in its infancy. Early designs spent most of their time on the surface, submerging only when in danger of attack. Torpedo and torpedo-aiming technology was also primitive. Success in battle depended more on the resourcefulness and daring of the U-boat's skipper than on technology or tactical doctrine. Nevertheless, U-boats took a heavy toll on British shipping, sinking nearly 10 million tons of cargo in two years, threatening Allied supply lines, and inflaming American public opinion. To combat the U-boats, the British began convoying and developing countermeasures.

To avoid detection, U-boats rarely used their transmitters. When they did, it was usually at night when there was less danger of being spotted on the surface. U-boat wireless operators used a low-frequency band to send short messages that were always coded. To triangulate their position, the British constructed radio directional stations along the coast of Britain. By taking cross bearings, these stations enabled operators to establish the position and, from successive positions, the course of any enemy vessel sending wireless signals, a process the British perfected during the Second World War.[13]

"Over there." - The US Enters the Great War

According to most historians, America entered the Great War in April 1917 because Germany had resumed unrestricted submarine warfare, sinking several American merchant vessels and the revelation of the German Zimmerman Telegram, which urged Mexico to attack the US in order to divert her attention away from Europe.[14]

In fact, the main reason America entered the war was because US banks had extended billions of dollars in loans to the Allied Powers, depositor monies they might not recover if the Allies lost the war. By April 1917, Russian morale was flagging. If Russia signed a ceasefire with Germany, the twenty-seven German divisions stationed on the eastern front would be free to deploy against the Allies in the west, heightening concerns that Allied armies would be overrun.

Photography

According to prewar military doctrine, the airplane's primary mission was aerial reconnaissance. By 1914 all major

---

[13] Called Huff-Duff, it laid the foundation for modern radar and radio navigation systems. Huff-Duff worked by detecting and pinpointing the direction of radio transmissions from enemy ships and submarines. By triangulating these signals, operators could accurately locate their source. Operating at high frequencies, Huff-Duff was particularly adept at detecting the short-range transmissions typical of submarines and surface vessels.

[14] British intelligence's Room 40 had intercepted Zimmerman's Telegram and gratefully passed it along to the Americans.

belligerents were equipped with aircraft and cameras. Because operating a camera while flying had proved impractical, special two-seat reconnaissance airplanes had been constructed with the pilot seated in the back and the observer in front. When enemy fighters appeared over the battlefield this configuration was quickly reversed to facilitate the installation of front and rear facing machine guns.[15]

Shortly after the United States entered the war in 1917, twenty-one-year-old Sherman Fairchild accompanied his father to Washington, DC, where they obtained a contract to develop an improved aerial camera. Sherman wanted to enlist but was rejected due to poor health. Sherman's father, George Fairchild, served six terms in the United States House of Representatives. He also served as Chairman of the Computing Tabulating Recording Company, later renamed International Business Machines (IBM). Sherman spent the $7,000 awarded by the US government and another $33,000 invested by his father, developing his first aerial camera. Although Sherman's camera did not see service during WWI, the US Army did purchase two units after the war for evaluation and training purposes.

Kodak's founder, George Eastman, was also quick to offer his company's services. Writing to the War Department in 1917, Eastman opined that:

"None of the Allies, and even Germany has, as you know, no organization which begins to cover the ground that ours does. The effectiveness of the work to be done practically depends entirely upon the close coordination of things that are already known. It is extremely unlikely that anything radically new will be discovered during the

---

[15] Fighters were first introduced to shoot down reconnaissance airplanes and balloons.

progress of this war and to coordinate these elements requires the work of the best experts in the world, which everybody acknowledges are centered in Rochester."

In March 1918, Eastman established the United States School of Aerial Photography at Kodak Park in Rochester, New York.

At war's end, the innovations developed for the military were incorporated into Kodak's consumer products and marketed internationally.

The Interwar Years - 1919 – 1939

When the armistice was signed in November 1918, the pace of technological advancements in radio, cryptology, and aeronautical design slowed. The war had drained the treasuries of the European belligerents, and there was little appetite for developing new military technologies. The US retreated into isolationism when the Senate rejected the Treaty of Versailles in 1919.[16] Economic conditions deteriorated with the onset of the Great Depression. It wasn't until Hitler came to power in 1933 and Germany began to rearm that state funding for new technologies resumed. Nevertheless, there were several notable developments during the interwar period. One of the most significant was broadcast radio.

When the US entered World War I in 1917, the few radios operating within its borders were owned by private hobbyists. The Navy ordered these systems shut down to maintain security and prevent private transmissions from

---

[16] This came as a surprise to the French, who had refrained from taking punitive measures to control the German economy based on President Wilson's pledge of American intervention through the League of Nations if Germany violated the treaty.

interfering with naval signal traffic. These restrictions were lifted when the war ended.

In most countries, early radio stations generated broadcasting revenues by selling sealed sets that could only receive pre-set frequencies. This restriction was akin to early cell phones locked to specific carrier networks. Just as savvy cell phone users found ways to unlock their phones, early radio enthusiasts built their own sets so they could tune to any channel within range.

After the war, every nation except America adopted a state-run broadcasting system. In the US, radio was funded by advertising revenues. Licensing fees for users were never introduced. Consequently, commercial radio broadcasting quickly expanded nationwide, providing listeners with a wide range of choices. Within ten years, most American families owned at least one radio. Independent broadcasters formed networks to share content, creating a syndicated programming market. In 1927, the government established the Federal Radio Commission, renamed the Federal Communications Commission (FCC) in 1934, to oversee the industry.

Reflecting on the different approaches to radio broadcasting and the results they produced, Judith Waller, director of Public Service at NBC, wrote in 1945 that there were fundamentally three radio systems: state-owned; the British Royal Charter system of an independent non-profit, public corporation; and the American commercial system. "In dictator-controlled countries," wrote Waller, "the objective of broadcasting is to give the people what the state wants them to have; in Great Britain, the objective seems to be to give the people what they ought to have; in America, broadcasters give the audience what it wants."

The first crude vacuum tubes were introduced in the mid-1920s. This innovation and follow-on refinements, such as improved speakers, revolutionized radio receivers and transmitters. Militaries in all countries soon transitioned from wired to improved wireless technologies, although wired systems persisted, primarily to provide enhanced security for behind-the-line communications.[17]

Aerial Reconnaissance

Between 1918 and 1939, the great powers retained and improved their aerial reconnaissance capabilities. Sherman Fairchild, encouraged by the two cameras he had sold to the US Army, established the Fairchild Aerial Camera Corporation in 1920 and began developing more advanced models.

Impressed with Sherman's improved camera, the Army purchased twenty units. Shortly thereafter, they selected Fairchild's design as their standard for aerial cameras.

In 1924, Sherman founded Fairchild Aviation Corporation which grew into one of America's leading aircraft manufacturers. During WWII, Fairchild participated in the aviation market mainly as a subcontractor with his Ranger Aircraft Engine subsidiary producing engines for the Navy. During World War II, over 90% of all aerial cameras used by Allied Forces were of Fairchild design or manufacture.

---

[17] At the dawn of the technology era, it was widely believed that each new technological advancement would render previous technologies obsolete. But this rarely happens. Usually, the prior technology finds a niche for which it is well-suited. For example, the radio was replaced mainly by TV in the home, but not in automobiles.

Moving Pictures

The interwar years were Hollywood's golden age. Five studios; Metro Goldwyn Mayer, RKO, 20th Century Fox, Warner Bros., and Paramount Pictures had a virtual lock on the motion picture industry, with Hollywood films – crafted primarily by foreign-born directors, dominating virtually all of the screen time in America, and the majority of screen time overseas. Movie theater attendance soared with the introduction of talkies and positively exploded during the Great Depression as care-worn Americans coughed up the few cents necessary to buy a ticket and escape their harsh economic reality – for a little while at least - by living vicariously through their favorite screen heroes.

The Cult of Personality

While neither still nor motion photography advanced much during the interwar years, the expansion of interwar technologies—including radio—sparked a social revolution that reverberates to the present day. Photographs had the power to move the masses in ways print never could. Every American is familiar with Joe Rosenthal's picture of five faceless marines raising a second, larger American flag on Mount Suribachi during the battle for Iwo Jima Island near the end of WWII.

Consumers queued up to purchase clothes in the styles worn by movie stars, history's first social influencers. Studios carefully groomed actors to appeal to mass audiences. In the 1920s, Charlie Chaplin was the most recognizable person on the planet. This cult of personality, a term coined by Soviet Premier Nikita Khrushchev in 1956, was a new phenomenon facilitated by advancements in mass media technologies. Political leaders from all countries were quick to bend these new technologies to their purpose. The

Nazis were masters of propaganda[18], using films such as Leni Riefenstahl's 1935 Triumph of the Will to portray Hitler as a godlike figure towering over the German people like Wotan in Wagner's Ring Cycle.

United States President Franklin Delano Roosevelt (FDR) used a series of radio broadcasts dubbed "fireside chats" to create an intimate setting where he could soothe the fears of Americans caught in the grip of the Great Depression.

The films *Why We Fight, With the Marines at Tarawa, The Fighting Lady, Memphis Belle, Combat America,* and *Winning Your Wings,* produced by the US government during WWII, are excellent examples of how America used Hollywood to galvanize the home front and prepare US troops for battle.[19]

Germany

Beginning in 1923, Winston Churchill, who had served as First Sea Lord of the British Navy from 1911 to 1915, published "The World Crisis," his five-volume "history" of the Great War. In it, he relates how the German light cruiser SMS Magdeburg, which ran aground off the island of Odensholm on August 26th, 1914, was seized by a pair of Russian cruisers. Three intact German code books, along with the current encryption key, were recovered in the assault. A few weeks later, the Russians passed their British allies one code book and the encryption key. Germany had long suspected that the Britain had been tipped off regarding

---

[18] Before being rebranded, propaganda was called "thought control."

[19] The US Defense Department frequently collaborates with Hollywood to produce films that portray military life positively in order to attract more recruits. A notable instance of this is the movie Top Gun, released in 1986, which inspired many young Americans to join the US Navy.

her movements during the Battles of Jutland and Dogger Bank. Still, the Germans attributed the leak to spies (human intelligence or HUMINT), not the breaking of their naval codes. Now, thanks to Churchill's indiscretion, they knew better.

This revelation, combined with contemporary advances in machine encryption, convinced the interwar German General Staff to abandon code books in favor of an electromechanical code machine. They selected a commercially available device, Enigma,[20] named by its inventor after "The Enigma Variations," a composition by British composer Sir Edward Elgar. To further enhance the device's security, the German military added a plugboard.

The Enigma machine that entered German military service in 1939 was the size of a large typewriter. Manufactured at the Skoda Works in Czechoslovakia, Enigma measured 13.5 by 11 by 6 inches, weighed twenty-six pounds and was powered by an internal 4.5-volt battery; although an outside power source could also be used. The keyboard had twenty-six letters arranged in a QWERTZ pattern. There were no keys for numerals or punctuation. Behind the keyboard was a lampboard containing twenty-six small circular windows, each bearing a letter arranged in the same QWERTZ pattern. Behind the lampboard was the scrambler unit, consisting of a fixed wheel at each end and a central space for inserting three of five available rotating wheels or rotors. Finally, the vertical front of the machine contained a plugboard with twenty-six pairs of sockets organized in the QWERTZ pattern. These were interconnected by ten twin-cable leads—for example, coupling G to J or L to H, etc. Six sockets were left

---

[20] Enigma is Greek for "puzzle."

unconnected. Throughout the war, successive refinements were introduced, varying from service to service, and there were detailed changes in operating procedures until 1945.

The genius of Enigma was in the vast number of crypto-variables or different combinations of encoding possibilities that it could generate. In choosing a basic set-up for the machine, there was a choice of 60 possible wheel orders, 17,576 ring settings for each wheel order, and over 150 738 274 937 250 plugboard pairings. For comparison, it is estimated that there are only 10 to the 79th power atoms in the observable universe.

Enigma was based on the same security model as current encryption technologies. Given the vast number of possible combinations and the technology available to plow through them, it was considered safe against any brute-force attack in which every possible combination is tried until the correct key is found. Just as AES 256 is deemed safe today, not because it can't be broken but because it would take too long to crack it with "known" technologies, the German military believed Enigma traffic was secure.[21]

Enter the Poles...

One of the Big Four's[22] most baffling decisions, when they met in France in 1919 to redraw the map of Europe, was the creation of the Polish Corridor. Their objective was to ensure Poland's economic prosperity by providing its people with access to the Baltic Sea. To achieve this aim, they split

[21] DARPA is significantly advancing quantum computing technology, which holds the potential to disrupt current encryption methods. Although quantum computing is still in its nascent stages, its future impact on code breaking is a crucial focus of research.

[22] The "Big Four" were: Woodrow Wilson, President of the United States; Georges Clemenceau, Prime Minister of France; David Lloyd George, Prime Minister of the United Kingdom; and Vittorio Orlando, Prime Minister of Italy.

Prussia, and established the free city of Danzig, effectively isolating East Prussia from the rest of Germany.

"Who will die for Danzig?" sneered the allied intelligentsia. In the end, tens of millions would die for Danzig.

Clearly, the leaders of the great powers, who crawled about on their hands and knees on the floor of a Versailles hotel room redrawing the map of Europe, had learned little about Prussian history from Frederick the Great, the Battle of Waterloo, Bismarck's reign, the influence wielded by Junkers within the German Officer Corps or Napoleon's observation that "Prussia was hatched from a cannonball."

When Hitler became Chancellor in 1933, he was determined to abrogate the Treaty of Versailles and unite all German-speaking peoples under one Reich.[23] Hitler regarded Danzig as an affront to German prestige and pressed for its reunification with Germany. In January 1939, he informed Polish Foreign Minister Josef Beck, "Danzig was German, would always remain German, and sooner or later would return to Germany." It is therefore not surprising that when the nervous Poles had the opportunity to examine a German Enigma machine, they jumped at the chance.

In January 1929, a package arrived in Warsaw addressed to the German Embassy. A customs officer was about to clear the heavy box for delivery when a German Embassy official, who insisted that the package had been sent by mistake, brusquely demanded its immediate release. Since the German official was rude and it was the weekend, his request was politely denied. When the incident was reported, a curious administrator ordered the crate pried

---

[23] The Holy Roman Empire was the first of three Reichs or Empires in German history. The second was the Hohenzollerns' Prussian- dominated empire forged by Bismarck. Hitler claimed his greater Germany was the Third.

opened, revealing an Enigma machine inside. The Polish General Staff's Cipher Bureau was immediately alerted and they dispatched two engineers who spent the rest of the weekend meticulously examining it. To keep their inspection secret, the engineers carefully repackaged the machine and ordered it delivered to the German Embassy Monday morning as scheduled.

Later, when Hitler was ratcheting up his anti-Polish propaganda campaign, the Polish General Staff's Cipher Bureau hired three promising Polish mathematicians to augment their existing brain trust. One of these men, Marian Rejewski, was able to work out which rotors were being used in the Enigma machine during a particular transmission but he still couldn't decipher messages because the Germans had used different wirings inside the rotors than those in the commercial Enigma the Poles had inspected previously.

Fortunately for Poland, a German named Hans Schmidt had walked into the French Embassy in Berlin about a year prior, claiming he worked in the German Cipher office and offered to sell them secrets. The French were suspicious, but when they confirmed that Schmidt's older brother, Rudolf, commanded the German Cipher office, they agreed to the purchase. Over the next several years, "Asché or Source D" provided hundreds of documents, including an Enigma instruction manual, detailed operating procedures, and lists of key settings. Even so, French Intelligence officers were still unable to break messages encrypted by Enigma; it was only when they shared this information with the Polish General Staff's Cipher Bureau that the breakthrough finally came. Rejewski had already devised a set of equations describing the operation of the then-new German Army Enigma rotor wirings. The key setting lists provided by Schmidt helped fill in enough of the unknowns in Rejewski's formulae to allow him to solve his equations and determine the wirings.

Armed with this new information, the Poles began clandestinely manufacturing copies of the Enigma machine. In 1938, Rejewski built a device he dubbed the bombe, which used eighteen rotors to test Enigma variations. This allowed the Poles to read approximately 75% of German Enigma traffic until the Germans introduced additional modifications in 1939.

While Poland labored to crack Enigma, the British and French Governments sought peace through appeasement. The most infamous incident occurred in Munich in 1938 when British and French leaders ceded the predominantly German-speaking Sudetenland to the Fuehrer based on his pledge that he would make no further territorial claims. When Germany seized the rest of Czechoslovakia just six months later, it was clear that Hitler's word could not be trusted. The only hope of avoiding war now was to impress upon the Führer that any further aggression would be met with force. Two weeks later, the British and the French did exactly that when they "guaranteed" Poland's borders.

Grasping the precariousness of the position they were in, Britain began preparing for war. This included collaborating with the Polish government, who, until the final months leading up to the war, also believed the best way to avoid conflict with the Germans was to avoid provoking them. They had, therefore, rebuffed overtures from the French and British to discuss a coordinated defense. The situation for the Poles became desperate during the last week of August 1939 when the Germans signed a non-aggression pact with the Soviet Union. Finally, with hostile forces massing on both their borders, the Poles shared their Enigma secrets with their French and British allies, including

Rejewski's bombe and copies of the machines they had manufactured. It was a good thing they did. Poland fell in four weeks, the British were swept off the continent the following summer and the French surrendered two weeks later. From this point until the German surrender in May 1945, the cracking of Enigma traffic would remain, almost entirely, a British endeavor.

World War II - Germany

On the evening of 31 August 1939, a small team of SS[24] men stormed the Gleiwitz Radio Station on the German border with Poland. Masquerading as Polish insurgents, they pushed past the German staff, seized the microphone, and announced in Polish: "Attention! This is Gleiwitz. This broadcasting station is now in Polish hands." To complete the ruse, the Germans drugged several concentration camp inmates and had them transported to the site. Dressed in Polish army uniforms and provided with Polish identifications, the inmates were shot, and their corpses left as evidence of the assault. The false flag operation, devised by Hitler's favorite Nazi, Reinhard Heydrich[25], was codenamed Operation Canned Goods. Outraged by this blatant act of Polish aggression, Germany invaded Poland early the next morning, plunging Europe into history's most destructive war. Four weeks later, with its army routed in the field and its capital Warsaw under constant land and air bombardment, Poland surrendered.

---

[24] The SS, or Schutzstaffel, originally served as Hitler's personal guard and evolved into a major paramilitary organization.

[25] The quintessential Aryan—cultured, tall, with blonde hair and blue eyes— Heydrich, head of Hitler's SD, is widely regarded as one of WWII's most sinister figures. It was Heydrich who provided Stalin with forged documents implicating senior Russian officers, leading Stalin to purge his military hierarchy in the lead-up to WWII.

The world was stunned by the speed of the German victory. The following summer, when the Germans defeated the Allied armies in Europe in just six weeks, a feat Imperial Germany had been unable to accomplish in four years, the world's press, unable to find an adequate vernacular descriptor, labeled this new type of quick war blitzkrieg.[26]

Blitzkrieg was a military tactic calculated to create psychological shock and resultant disorganization in enemy forces by employing surprise, speed, and superiority in materiel or firepower. As the German Condor Legion learned in the Spanish Civil War proving ground, radio was the key to effective Blitzkrieg operations. Accordingly, every German tank, plane, and ground unit was equipped with a radio, enabling commanders to coordinate attacks. To keep command directives secret, the Germans relied principally on two coding machines: Enigma for everyday field-based operations and the more sophisticated Lorenz SZ, used exclusively by the German High Command.

The Battle of Britain

In the summer of 1940, Enigma decrypts revealed that "[s]ince England, in spite of her hopeless military situation, shows no signs of being ready to come to a compromise, I [Hitler] have decided to prepare a landing operation against England, and, if necessary, to carry it out."[27] The British braced for the air battle they knew must shortly begin, for they understood, just as the Germans did, that unless the Luftwaffe achieved air superiority over the channel, the Wehrmacht could not hope to land forces on the English

---

[26] Lightening War. "Speed of attack through speed of communications." — German Field Marshal Erhard Milch, who supervised the development of the Luftwaffe.

[27] Adolph Hitler, July 1940

coast. Fortunately for the British, they had several factors in their favor.

First, the Royal Navy. In the summer of 1940, the British possessed the world's largest and most formidable navy. Airpower aside, the Royal Navy would have most fiercely contested any German foray into the English Channel.

Second, Radio Direction Finding (RDF) or, as we refer to it today, radar. In contrast to early radio, radar was developed in a partnership between the military and private sector. While several scientists in different countries contributed to its development, most historians attribute its invention to Britain's Robert Watson-Watt. In 1935, Watt wrote a paper entitled 'Detection and Location of Aircraft by Radio Methods.' Two weeks later, in a joint experiment conducted with the RAF, Watt's apparatus detected a Hadley Page Bomber from eight miles away.[28] British Air Ministry officials and Royal Air Force officers who attended the demonstration were suitably impressed. The British government made funds available, and by 1938, Watt and his expanded team had developed a serviceable device.[29]

The third of Britain's advantages was a tightly integrated air defense network; and its fourth, the right man to head it; Air Chief Marshal Hugh Dowding. Nicknamed "Stuffy" by his men, Dowding eschewed socializing, drank very little, believed in spiritualism, and, in his later years, advocated for animal rights. But in the late 1930s, Dowding was the right man in the right place. In contrast to most Royal Air Force (RAF) officers, Dowding possessed both a

---

[28] Initially, Watt had been trying to develop a death ray capable of debilitating enemy fliers in their cockpits.

[29] Think of radar like cameras. Both are essentially sensors, ways in which machines experience reality.

technical and theoretical understanding of modern air warfare. A flier with the Royal Air Corp during WWI, Dowding was the first Briton to receive radio signals in the air.

Dowding understood that radar could detect the Luftwaffe, but not stave it off. To do that, he would need to incorporate Watt's invention with Britain's earlier air defense efforts, such as the observer core with its primitive command and control systems. He would also need new fighters able to go head to head with Germany's Messerschmitt Bf 109s. Dowding set to work welding the requisite components into the world's first integrated defense network.

Dowding's system connected people, radar and communications technology to detect attacks and coordinate responses. Early warning radar stations, code-named Chain Home, were constructed up and down the British coast. This coverage was later augmented by Chain Home Low, an ancillary series of radar stations designed to spot enemy planes trying to avoid detection by flying low to the water.[30] By the summer of 1940, British radar operators could detect German planes the moment they lifted off from their bases in France, including their course, altitude, and approximate numbers. This information was telephoned to a Filter Room with a large map table that would filter out extraneous information, such as friendly airplanes or German civilian air traffic. If officers in the Filter Room determined a raid was forming up, a teller passed the specifics to the central Operations Room at Fighter Command. The information was also shared with the affected Group and its Sector stations. Group Controllers watched the raid develop on their map tables, decided how best to allocate their squadrons, and

---

[30] A tactic from which the idiom "under the radar" was derived.

telephoned instructions to their Sector stations. Since plotters at the Sector stations followed the raid on their own map tables, they were ready to scramble as soon as the Sector Controller gave the order.

Once the squadrons were airborne, ground controllers vectored them toward their targets. When the enemy was sighted, the squadron leader radioed that he was attacking. This information was then updated on tote boards[31] located at Command, Group, and Sector stations.

Air battles were typically brief, usually lasting less than ten minutes, with surviving fighters, their fuel and ordnance depleted, ordered to land. Since by this time, the raiders would most likely have passed over the coast, they were now invisible to British radar, which pointed out to sea. This is where the Observer Core (OC), primarily civilians equipped with basic tools for determining course and altitude, took over. Like their radar operator counterparts, they would telephone their information to OC filter stations networked with Fighter Command, and the process would start all over again. To further complicate operations, anti-aircraft batteries were similarly controlled by Fighter command.

Like the German blitzkrieg, Dowding's defense system relied on communications for success. From the time a raid formed up over France until it arrived over Britain could take as little as twenty minutes. Since a British fighter climbed 2,000 feet a minute, and it had to ascend to at least 15,000 feet to have any chance of intercepting the German planes, the ground controllers had only minutes to determine the size and course of a raid, decide how many

---

[31] The different colored lights on the tote board provided the fighter controller with an instant visual indication of the state of the fighter squadrons at his disposal, at each of the Sector airfields.

fighters to dispatch to meet it and issue scramble orders to the appropriate squadrons.

This was the real magic that Dowding accomplished: the cobbling together of the first truly integrated air defense network, the computerized model of which exists to the present day. It was an analog network, to be sure, but a network nonetheless. It used human and electronic sensors to detect and track threats, manual plotting tables and electric tote boards to record progress, human intelligence to filter information, and networked telephone and radio communications to link together all of its nodes on the ground and in the air.

The final key to Dowding's air defense network's success was the introduction of two superb single-seat, monoplane fighters: the Hawker Hurricane and R.J. Mitchell's Spitfire.[32] Introduced in 1937 and 1939, the combination fabric and metal Hurricane was based on an earlier Hawker design, while the Spitfire was an all-metal aircraft. Both machines were powered by the legendary Rolls Royce V12 "Merlin" engine and equipped with radios.

In addition to fighters, both sides entered the war equipped with advanced multi-engine bombers[33] and disparate theories, advocated by prominent air force theorists, on how best to use them. Two of the most influential were Italian Giulio Douhet and American Billy

---

[32] A little-known but fascinating story is that Lady Houston, a wealthy British socialite and aviation enthusiast, played a crucial role in developing the Spitfire during the 1930s. Recognizing the growing tensions in Europe and the need for advanced military aircraft, Lady Houston funded the project when the parsimonious British Air Ministry refused to provide the necessary funds.

[33] It is important to note here that the Germans possessed only medium-range bombers, while the British had both medium-range and long-range bombers. The British would press home this advantage with ever greater ferocity until the war's end in 1945.

Mitchell. Douhet and Mitchell understood that the Great War marked a turning point in how wars were fought and fervently believed that any future wars could not be won without control of the air. They further postulated that since civilian-based industry produced the material necessary to wage wars, factories and their workers were legitimate targets. Both officers were persecuted by their respective services for publicly expressing such unchivalrous views. Still, by the mid-1930s, their theories had found their way into the mainstream; air technology was rapidly evolving, and there was a belief on both sides that any future war would undoubtedly involve the mass bombing of cities - perhaps with poison gas - and that no matter how efficient a country's air defenses, "the bomber would always get through."[34]

Enigma

Ultra-secret intelligence obtained from Enigma, codenamed "Ultra," was Britain's most closely guarded secret of the war. Ultra impacted the Campaign in the Desert, the Air War over Europe, the Battle of the Atlantic, and Operation Overlord.

World War I cryptologist Dilly Knox led the British effort to crack Enigma. Partnering with Tony Kendrick, Knox established "Station X" at Bletchley Park, an ornate country house in Buckinghamshire England. There they were joined by Peter Twinn, Alan Turing, and Gordon Welchman. Piggybacking off of Polish and French efforts, Bletchley was able to crack a small amount of code by January 1940.

In October 1941, Turing and Welchman coauthored a letter addressed to then Prime Minister Winston Churchill,

---

[34] From Stanley Baldwin's 1932 speech to British members of Parliament.

opining that unless additional staff were provided immediately, the work would be held up or not done at all. Like Dowding before them, Turing and Welchman realized that fully exploiting Enigma-based intelligence required thousands of workers to do all manner of essential jobs. They also needed a secure communications network to facilitate traffic between the operation's many divisions to ensure the Enigma secret was never compromised.[35]

For his part, Welchman realized that much could be gained from studying the unencrypted elements of intercepted messages, a practice analogous to analyzing the information on the outside of an envelope. This mapping of German radio traffic, now referred to as "traffic analysis," was such a powerful intelligence technique that its use remained classified long after other Bletchley Park secrets were revealed. Edward Snowden shed further light on the practice in 2013 when he revealed that security agencies use metadata - data about data - to track where you go, when, and with whom you meet. By tracking your phone, the intelligence operatives can see where you work, and by tracking the phones of those around you, where and with whom you spend your off-hours. They can also learn a lot about you from the websites you visit. In fact, traffic analysis is so powerful that there is rarely a need to access the content of your private conversations. More importantly for State-run security agencies, no warrants are required since intelligence officers never actually open your mail and read the contents and therefore, are not "technically" violating your privacy.

Using traffic analysis, Bletchley Park could pinpoint enemy headquarters, the location of forward bases, when

---

[35] And thus the bureaucracy of the modern surveillance state was born.

they advanced or retreated, and, based on the amount of traffic, whether or not something was stirring on a particular front. Most importantly, since success in war depends on getting intelligence to theatre commanders before latency renders it worthless, traffic analysis helped British codebreakers determine which intercepted messages to prioritize for decryption.

Alan Turing's major contribution to unraveling Enigma was his conviction that cracking the daily rotor settings could be expedited by a machine. Turing realized that the existing process of finding a crib and racing to work out the code's key before the Germans changed it the following day was too slow and haphazard: speed and consistency meant lives.

And yet, despite widespread belief to the contrary, the machine that Alan Turing designed was not powerful enough to crack the daily rotor settings by plowing serially through every possible combination, even after incorporating the intelligent design features suggested by Welchman. The crib remained an essential part of the process.

For those unacquainted with the arcane world of codebreaking, a crib is an insight that can be leveraged to narrow down the number of possible crypto keys. For example, if a German operator ends every transmission with Heil Hitler, then the codebreakers could tune Turing's machine to find the key that would produce the word "Hitler" from a single string of code rather than plowing through an entire message until an intercept became intelligible. Armed with a crib, Turing's machine could be calibrated or "programmed" to exploit it, reducing machine runs from hours to minutes. Turing called his machine a cryptologic bombe after the rudimentary device designed by Rejewski for the same purpose.

In contrast to Rejewski's device, which was about the size of a toaster, Turing's bombe was a giant electromechanical machine seven feet tall, ten feet wide, and three feet deep. It weighed 5,000 pounds and was mounted on large rollers. On its front were rows of tri-color drums wired up in the same configuration as an Enigma machine. Each drum had twenty-six positions corresponding to the letters on the Enigma rotors and keyboard. When the twenty-sixth letter was reached, the contiguous drum would click over the same way an odometer does in a car. The plugboard, which mimicked the plugboard on the Enigma, was located on the back of the machine. Bombe operators would "tune" the plugboard settings based on a "menu" that codebreakers produced from a crib.[36] Once the settings were double-checked, the machines were started. The drums clicked round, letter by letter, testing the thousands of possible enigma settings, 20 every second until a possible setting was found. Once all three drums stopped, an operator recorded the settings and passed them into an adjoining office, where they were tested on an Enigma copy. If this machine successfully deciphered a test message, the run was concluded and the key passed to the decoders who went to work on that day's message traffic. Finally, the decrypted messages were translated from German to English and forwarded to British intelligence officers for action.

Turing's bombe transformed Station X from a small-scale operation to an industrial enterprise. British signals intelligence collection sites, codenamed Y-stations, were set up all over Britain to intercept and transcribe German

---

[36] Plugboard technology was later incorporated into the first computers to make reprogramming faster.

Enigma traffic. The transcripts were forwarded to Bletchley by secure courier or teletype. Separate buildings or "huts" shadowed the various German Service Arms - each service employed its own Enigma configuration - and harvested their cribs. When a practicable crib could not be found, codebreakers "seeded" enemy radio traffic by requesting a plane to knock out a specific target, such as a German reporting station, knowing full well the operators would report the damage and identify the station's name in their message. The British called this process "gardening."[37]

Shark

By 1941, Bletchley Park was regularly decrypting Enigma traffic between German U-boats stationed in the Atlantic and their new headquarters in Lorient. This intelligence was used to route convoys away from German "Wolf" packs. Convinced there was a breach in security, Admiral Doenitz, Commander of the German Navy, ordered the addition of a fourth rotor in 1942. Bletchley codenamed the new cipher Shark. Fortunately for the British, the fourth rotor was one of two types, Beta or Gamma, which didn't step; it was manually set to any one of 26 positions. Consequently, codebreakers had only to determine which of the 26 positions was in use on a particular day and set the rotor, after which the machine performed identically to a three-rotor enigma. Once Bletchley figured this out, they added a fourth rotor to their triple logic bombes. However, these early bombes proved too slow, and the British lacked

---

[37] In 1942, the US Navy employed "gardening" to identify AF as Midway Island. A Midway radio operator sent an unencrypted message about the island's broken fresh water condensers. This led a Japanese radio operator to code a message about AF being low on fresh water. American codebreakers in Hawaii intercepted this coded message, confirming that AF was indeed Midway.

the resources to keep up with current demands and build new ones. The problem was solved by turning Shark over to the United States Navy. Building on Turing's bombe, US mathematicians drew up next-generation designs. The new machines were engineered and built at National Cash Register (NCR) in Dayton, Ohio, and installed in the US Naval Communications Annex in Washington D.C. By the end of the war, there were over 200 bombes in Britain and the United States turning out 90,000 decoded messages a month.

Lorenz Z

Beginning in 1940, the German High Command used a teletypewriter in-line cipher machine with twelve rotors for its highest-priority traffic. Called a Lorenz Z, it was more advanced, faster, and more secure than Enigma. Code-named "Fish" by Bletchley, Lorenz worked by surrounding encoded letters with extraneous text arrayed in a single unbroken string. In contrast to Enigma, Fish was broken exclusively using a statistical technique of code-breaking.

In any language, certain letters appear more frequently than others. Based on this anomaly and an operator error, in which a German cipher clerk transmitted the same message twice using the same rotor settings, Bletchley was able to decrypt the code and build a machine that could duplicate it. The WAAFs[38] christened the strange-looking contraption "Heath Robinson" after an English cartoonist best known for his whimsical drawings of elaborate machines. The design was improved on later by Tommy Flowers, an engineer recruited from the British Post

---

[38] The Women's Auxiliary Air Force (WAAF), whose members were referred to as WAAFs was the female auxiliary of the British Royal Air Force during World War II.

Office, who advocated a vacuum tube-based design that analyzed punched paper tape via an optical reader. Codenamed Colossus, [39]ten machines were constructed and in constant use at war's end.[40]

V-1 Flying Bomb

In 1939, The German Army allocated funds to develop an unmanned flying bomb. Dubbed the V-1[41], the weapon employed a pair of gyroscopes to control pitch and yaw and a magnetic compass to maintain azimuth. A barometric device controlled altitude, and an odometer, calibrated before launch to compensate for prevailing winds, counted backward to measure the distance to the target. When the counter reached zero, the engines cut out, and the V-1 plunged to earth.

Germany's V-1 was the world's first operational cruise missile. Later in the war, experiments were conducted where V-1s were fitted with radios to control them remotely.[42] In this configuration, V-1s also laid the foundation of contemporary drone technologies.

For example, Lockheed's D-21 was an American-built supersonic reconnaissance drone shaped like a 44-foot manta ray. It could reach speeds exceeding Mach 3.3 at altitudes of up to 90,000 feet and had a smaller radar cross-section than any previous aircraft. The D-21 was designed to carry a high-

---

[39] Colossus was chosen as the name of the computer that took over the world in the 1970 movie Colossus – The Forbin Project.

[40] All but two of the Colossus machines were dismantled in 1945. The remaining computers were used by the UK's Government Communications Headquarters (GCHQ) to decrypt Soviet messages until the 1960s.

[41] V-1 or "Vengeance Weapon 1".

[42] The USAAF conducted a similar experiment using radio controlled B-17s packed with explosives with disastrous results. Joseph Kennedy Jr. was killed during one such operation.

resolution photographic camera and fly a preprogrammed path. After exposing its film, the D-21 ejected the camera module, which was retrieved in mid-air by a specially modified JC-130 Hercules. The D-21 self-destructed once its mission was completed to keep it from falling into enemy hands.

Kelly Johnson[43] of Lockheed's Skunk Works developed the D-21 for the CIA in October 1962 but due to the CIA's focus on U-2 missions, the project was temporarily shelved. When the USAF expressed interest in the technology, the CIA revived the project, and work recommenced in March 1963.

Despite trial successes, operational launches between 1969 and 1971 to photograph the People's Republic of China's Lop Nor nuclear test site yielded poor results. With the advent of satellite technology, the D-21 became redundant, and the project was canceled.

V-2 Rocket

The V-2[44] ballistic missile was the world's first operational liquid-fuel rocket. Germany's Ordnance Department funded its initial development. The V2 was Germany's most expensive war program, costing some $2 billion in 1944 dollars. Three thousand two hundred twenty-five were launched in combat, primarily at London and later against the main Allied supply port in Antwerp. The V-2 rocket laid the foundation for the Saturn V rocket, which launched the Apollo astronauts to the moon.[45]

---

[43] Clarence "Kelly" Johnson was most probably the greatest airplane designer in history, having designed the Lockheed P-38 Lightning, the SR-71 Blackbird, and the U-2 spy plane.

[44] Second in the series of Vengeance Weapons, the V-2 or "Retribution Weapon 2."

Me-262 (Jet Propulsion)

The Messerschmitt Me 262 was the world's first operational jet-powered fighter aircraft. Jet propulsion and swept-back wings opened the door to speeds beyond Mach 1 by pushing the aircraft through the air rather than screwing or pulling it, as is the case with propeller-driven aircraft. Jet engine technology was developed between the wars in both Britain and Germany by Frank Whittle and Hans Joachim Pabst von Ohai. There is no evidence that they were aware of each other's research. Jet propulsion research proceeded slowly until the Governments of Britain and Germany provided funding following the outbreak of war in 1939.

The Rising Sun - Japan 1853 -1941

To understand Japanese politics from the end of the 19th century until Nippon's defeat in 1945, one needs to start with the visit of four American warships to Edo[46] on July 8, 1853, under the command of Commodore Matthew Perry. The visit was intended to establish diplomatic relations between the US and Japan. The United States had several compelling reasons for wanting to do so.

Opening Chinese ports to regular trade ensured a steady stream of maritime traffic between North America and Asia. As steam replaced sail, coaling stations were needed where ships could take on the additional fuel and provisions necessary to make the long trip. Additionally, insatiable American whalers had pushed into the North Pacific by the mid-19th century and sought safe harbors and assistance in case of shipwrecks. In the years leading up to

---

[45] Both the V-2 and the Saturn 5 rockets were developed by Wernher von Braun and his team of German scientists.

[46] In 1868, the Tokugawa Shogunate ended and Imperial Rule was restored. The Emperor moved to Edo which was then renamed Tokyo.

the Perry mission, an increasing number of American sailors were shipwrecked on Japanese shores. Their salacious tales of "barbarous" treatment at the hands of Japanese "infidels" fueled animosity within America's merchant community and in Washington.

When Commodore Perry arrived bearing gifts in four black warships[47] and trained his massive guns on Edo, Japanese officials were more awed by the guns than the gifts. Essentially, the Japanese were presented with two choices: they could ignore America's invitation to join the community of nations - in which case they could expect to end up like the Chinese where the Great Powers dominated all aspects of the government and economy - or adopt the technologies employed by the West to springboard Imperial Japan into the modern age. The Japanese plumped for the latter. Specifically, they chose to model their Navy on the British, their army on the Prussians, and their Government on Britain's Parliamentary system - with one crucial exception: the Japanese Prime Minister did not necessarily control the majority of seats in the Diet. The Emperor appointed him. Consequently, he and his cabinet were not constrained by the voice of Parliament. In this regard, the Japanese Government functioned more like pre-WWI Imperial Germany than Great Britain. And within a few years, they displayed the same predatory instincts.

In 1895, the Japanese Army fought with China over Korea and took control of Taiwan and the Penghu Islands. In 1905, the Imperial Japanese Navy annihilated the Russian battle fleet in forty minutes in the battle of Tsushima. Japan's

---

[47] In 1907, President Theodore Roosevelt ordered the United States Navy's Atlantic Fleet, consisting of 16 battleships, to be painted white. This distinctive color scheme was intended to symbolize peace and goodwill during its historic world tour.

greatest contribution to the Allied War effort in WWI was seizing Germany's Pacific colonies. By 1919, there was growing fear in the West, especially in America, that the Japanese constituted a threat to Western interests in the Pacific, in the same way that China is regarded as the principal threat today.

To ease tensions and avoid an arms race, the Americans convoked a Five Power[48] conference in Washington in 1922 to establish maximum allowable naval tonnages. While the Americans were pleased with the conference's outcome, the Japanese were not. For Japan, the 1922 Washington Naval Treaty marked the third time Japan's request for parity with the other Great Powers had been rebuffed.

The first was The Treaty of Portsmouth, which formally ended the 1904–05 Russo-Japanese War and was signed at the Portsmouth Naval Shipyard in Kittery, Maine. US President Theodore Roosevelt, who played a leading role in the negotiations, won the Nobel Peace Prize for his efforts. However, the treaty was not well-received by the Japanese people, who were generally unaware that their negotiators were forced to make concessions due to Japan's unsustainable overextension of military and economic resources. Exhilarated by their unbroken string of military victories, the Japanese people viewed the settlement, which returned portions of conquered lands to their enemy, as inexplicable. There were riots in the streets, and Prime Minister Katsura Tarō's government fell.

The second came in 1919 during the Paris peace talks when "The Racial Equality Proposal," an amendment proposed by the Japanese to abolish racial discrimination

---

[48] The five powers were the United States, Great Britain, Japan, France, and Italy.

among members of the League of Nations, was rejected based on opposition from the United States and Australia.

The third, and in the eyes of Japanese nationalists, the most inimical to their interests was - as already pointed out - the Washington Naval Limitation Treaty. The treaty allotted 500,000 tons to the United States and the United Kingdom and 300,000 tons to Japan. The reasoning provided by the West for this inequity was that in contrast to the Japanese, the British and Americans required "two ocean" navies to defend their borders and protect their overseas interests.[49] That these forces could, and most probably would, be conjoined in the event of any future dispute between the signatories was not lost on the Japanese.

"Strange thing is they make such bloody good cameras." - Dr. Strangelove (1964)

In 1922, the Japanese believed the Great Powers were an English-led, white-only club that would never accept Japan as an equal, despite their punctiliousness in applying the same imperialist practices by which the Great Powers had established their Empires.[50] Japanese resentment was further aggravated when Herbert Yardley, an American cryptologist, published "The American Black Chamber" in 1931. Yardley's book revealed how the US had intercepted and decoded the diplomatic traffic between Japan and its

---

[49] The Japanese delegates were perturbed by the fact that 20 years previous, the British Parliament had passed the Naval Defense Act in 1889 which formally adopted a "two-power standard" calling for the Royal Navy to maintain a number of battleships at least equal to the combined strength of the next two largest navies.

[50] Racism against the Japanese persisted long after World War II ended in 1945. The Sony Corporation, which later became a global leader in electronics, chose the name "Sony" as a subtle response to American G.I.s who derisively referred to Japanese men as "Sonny boy."

delegates during the Washington-based naval negotiations in 1921. Consequently, US negotiators knew that Tokyo had instructed its Japanese delegates to back down if the talks reached an impasse. Accordingly, the Americans offered no concessions.

Tokyo was outraged—and rightly so. Eavesdropping on the private conversations of delegates who are met together in good faith to negotiate terms by which nations can harmoniously coexist raises troubling concerns.

In 1921, Japan had not threatened Western interests. Japan and America were at peace. Using surveillance to determine the minimal demands of another party is not good bargaining practice; it is chicanery. Worse, the US Government ordered the American Telephone and Telegraph Company (AT&T), a private company, to provide them with access to Japanese telephone calls and telegrams. Obviously, there was little purpose in listening in on Japanese communications if the Japanese knew the Americans were doing so. So, what legal instrument did the Government use to obtain these extraordinary powers? Certainly, they did not make the request in open court. Was Congress apprised of what they were doing or was it merely a decision taken by senior government officials in a clandestine meeting? Given the documents leaked by Edward Snowden, which revealed the "highly collaborative" relationship between the NSA (of which Yardley's group was a predecessor) and telecom giant AT&T, which provided "massive amounts of data" about American citizens to the US government between 2003 and 2013 - including billions of emails, these issues and the concerns they raise are just as relevant today.

Both the US and Britain retained their Signals Intelligence Departments after the Great War ended.

However, in 1924, the American government halved the department's budget. Five years later, rocked by the Great Depression, they shut it down. This decision coincided with Henry Stimson's appointment as Secretary of State. State was a co-funder of the Signals Intelligence Department. At the time, it was reported that Stimson, a man much respected for his moral rectitude, closed it because "gentlemen do not read each other's mail." This explanation, however, is probably apocryphal. More likely, the department was closed for economic reasons. In the 1920s and thirties, the US Government did not have the same intrusive access to private earnings that it does today, and the majority of Americans still looked upon standing armies with the same suspicion as their founding fathers. Consequently, defense budgets were drastically paired back between wars.

All of this changed in the 1930s with the rise of fascism on the Continent and blatant Japanese adventurism in Northeastern China. On September 18, 1931, Japanese Army officers blew up a section of their own railway, blamed Chinese nationalists, and then "retaliated" by invading Manchuria. The League of Nations conducted an inquiry that condemned the Japanese as aggressors.[51] The Japanese quit the League in protest. The US responded with the Stimson Doctrine, a policy of non-recognition of international territorial changes executed by force,[52] and began ramping up their Signals Intelligence Service (SIS).

The Army's SIS was headed by William Friedman, considered by many to be the most influential cryptologist—a classification he coined—of all time. Freidman and his wife

---

[51] The Lytton report stated that Japan was the aggressor, had wrongfully invaded Manchuria and that it should be returned to the Chinese.
[52] Based on an application of the principle of ex injuria jus non oritur, "Unjust acts cannot create law".

Elizabeth, a brilliant cryptologist in her own right, got their start working for "Colonel" George Fabyan,[53] an American millionaire businessman who founded his own private research laboratory. Together, Bill and Elizabeth conducted research into the works of William Shakespeare, which Fabyan believed were written by Sir Francis Bacon, who had allegedly hidden clues to his authorship in the various texts. In their spare time, William wrote several ground-breaking papers on the study of cryptography, collectively known as the "Riverbank Publications,"[54] while Elizabeth deciphered mob accounting ledgers for the Treasury Department during Prohibition.

In the 1930s the SIS began experimenting with rotor-based machines for encryption. Friedman strongly believed that to crack complex code, you first had to be able to create it. He and his team created SIGABA, the US's highest-security cipher machine. The SIS also picked up where Yardley left off, recruiting mathematicians and navy signal officers with Japanese language skills to crack Japanese military and diplomatic codes.

In 1939 the Japanese introduced their first cipher machine to encrypt diplomatic traffic. Codenamed PURPLE by the SIS, Friedman and his team set about determining how the machine worked. By the end of 1940, in a brilliant feat of codebreaking, they had constructed an exact analog of the PURPLE machine.

In July 1937 the simmering pot that typified Japanese-Sino relations boiled over, when the Japanese army invaded

---

[53] Fabyan held no military rank. Rather, "Colonel" was a sobriquet bestowed by Southerners on distinguished elderly men. Colonel House, Woodrow Wilson's closest advisor, is a prominent example of this application.

[54] Fabyan's Chicago estate was named Riverbank. His research complex, housed on the same site, was named Riverbank Laboratories.

mainland China. In December the Japanese army fought their way into Nanjing, where they embarked on a brutal campaign of rape and mass murder of hundreds of thousands of Chinese civilians. That same month Japanese airmen attacked and sank the gunboat U.S.S. Panay, despite the US flags prominently painted on both sides of her deck. In June of 1940 FDR ordered the Pacific Fleet, anchored in San Diego, to Hawaii, 2200 miles closer to Japan. On August 1 Japanese Foreign Minister Yōsuke Matsuoka outlined Japan's vision of an Asian Co-Prosperity Sphere, a clear signal to Westerners that Japan envisioned an Asia dominated by Asians. The regions of Asia, Matsuoka argued, were as essential to Japan as Latin America was to the United States.[55]

On September 22, 1940 the Japanese took advantage of Germany's defeat over France to occupy French Indochina. Japan's objective was to prevent China from importing American arms and fuel from the Indochinese port of Haiphong, through the capital of Hanoi, to the Chinese city of Kunming in Yunnan. The United States responded four days later, declaring an embargo on scrap metal shipments to Japan effective October 15, 1940. The following day, Japanese Ambassador Saburō Kurusu signed the Tripartite Pact in Berlin.[56] On April 13, 1941, the Japanese followed Germany's lead and signed a Neutrality Pact with the Soviet Union. Two days later, President Roosevelt signed an

---

[55] Not completely dissimilar to the Monroe Doctrine, laid down by President James Monroe in 1823, which states that any intervention by external powers in the politics of the Americas is a potentially hostile act against the US

[56] The Pact was clearly aimed at the United States. It stipulated that if any Axis power was attacked by another country that had not joined the war, such as the United States or the Soviet Union (with whom Germany had already signed a non-aggression agreement), all the other signatories would come to their defense.

unpublicized executive order permitting reserve officers and enlisted men to resign from the US Army Air Force, Navy, and Marine Air Services to join the Flying Tigers, an all-American Volunteer Group (AVG) commanded by Claire Chennault who were training in Burma to take on the Japanese Air Force. On July 26th, 1941, FDR froze Japan's US assets. Five days later, he placed an embargo on all gasoline and oil exports to Japan. The following month, the US forbade Japanese use of the Panama Canal.

It was the oil embargo that set the countdown to war ticking. The Japanese had almost no reserves or refining capabilities and, therefore, relied heavily on imports for domestic use and fueling their massive war machine.[57] In 1941 the vast majority of these imports came from the United States. The only alternative was the oil produced in the Dutch East Indies, but this option had also been denied to the Japanese through embargo.

Americans were outraged at Japanese aggression in China and demanded action. The Japanese were willing to negotiate their position in Indochina. They were also willing to address US concerns over Japan's participation in the Axis via the Tripartite Pact, a document that US Secretary of State Cordell described as "nothing less than an agreement between the Germans and the Japanese to divide the world between them." But on China, the Japanese were unwilling to bend.

The Japanese had been fighting in China for four years, suffering over 100,000 casualties and expending vast amounts of treasure. To maintain support for the war, the Japanese people had been force-fed a steady diet of ultra-

---

[57] Oil is the lifeblood of the military. Until ships, tanks, trucks, and fighters are powered by solar energy, a war in the Middle East is more likely to trigger a global apocalypse than a conflict in any other region.

nationalist propaganda. Pulling out without establishing an "honorable" peace would cause the Japanese nation to lose face and bring down the government.[58]

The Japanese had only two choices: leave China or go to war with the world's most powerful industrial nation. In eighteen months Japan's oil reserves would be exhausted, and she would be forced to capitulate. Both sides made concerted efforts to resolve the impasse.

Ironically, the Japanese intercepts decrypted by Washington made the situation murkier. The US State Department knew Tokyo was preparing for war so they tended to discount any Japanese overture, no matter how sincere. The Japanese, unable to fathom why the Americans showed such little interest in what they considered major concessions, concluded that the US was stalling until Japanese fuel reserves were spent.[59]

And so, the Japanese generals prepared for war. On November 4, 1941 Emperor Hirohito approved the government's war plan: Japan would destroy the American fleet at Pearl Harbor. With the US Fleet neutralized, the Imperial Japanese Navy (IJN) and Army would be free to seize the resource-rich lands of Southeast Asia. Once they solved their resource challenges, the Japanese would strengthen their outer defense ring and make peace overtures to the Americans. With a bit of luck, it would all be over in six months.

The table was set. The doomsday clock in the East began ticking down.

---

[58] The United States found itself in a similar situation 30 years later in Vietnam.

[59] Marshall and King had indeed urged FDR to prolong discussions with the Japanese, hoping that the delay would give the US more time to prepare for war.

World War II – Japan

On Dec. 6, 1941 the US Army's Signal Intelligence Service (SIS) intercepted a long message from the Japanese government to its Washington, D.C. delegation. SIS decrypted the first thirteen parts of the message, which detailed Japanese claims of American transgressions in the Far East. At 5 a.m. December 7, 1941 the fourteenth and final part of the message arrived: "The Japanese Government regrets to have to notify the American Government that in view of the attitude of the American Government it cannot but consider that it is impossible to reach an agreement through further negotiations."

Because the Japanese transmitted the fourteen-part message using PURPLE, which the SIS had copied more than a year previous, intelligence officers were able to decode the message and get it into the hands of Washington officials several hours before Japanese diplomats were scheduled to present it to the American Secretary of State. However, unlike Bletchley in 1940, Washington in 1941 did not yet possess the bureaucracy necessary to collate, analyze, and effectively distribute decrypts obtained through its "MAGIC"[60] program. Consequently, Fort Shafter, Hawaii, did not receive the message until 11:45 a.m. By the time it was decoded and delivered to the Adjutant General's Office three hours later, thousands of US military personnel and civilians were dead, the US battleship fleet had been virtually destroyed, and the carriers that mounted the attack were steaming back to Japan.

But SIGINT was not the Army's only failure that morning; two privates at the Opana radar station in Hawaii

---

[60] MAGIC was the codename for the United States' project to intercept, decrypt, and analyze Japanese diplomatic communications during World War II.

detected the incoming Japanese planes while they were still about an hour away. The excited operators called the information center at Fort Shafter. It was a Sunday morning, and the center was empty except for a young Lieutenant who was the acting duty officer. He assumed it was a flight of B17s scheduled to arrive that morning from the mainland and told the privates not to worry about it. The operators switched off the set and went for breakfast.

JN-25

JN-XX[61] was the classification schema used by American cryptologists to catalog Japan's successive codes for encrypting radio traffic throughout the interwar years and World War II. Although the Japanese frequently modified their codes, there is no evidence to suggest they ever suspected they had been compromised, with the exception of JN-39, which was quickly replaced by JN-40.[62] Every JN code was eventually broken.

The JN codes consisted of two books: the first contained the code used for encryption, while the second included an additive cipher applied to the codes before transmission. The starting point for this additive cipher was embedded within the transmitted message itself.

To accelerate the decryption process, Washington's OP-G-20 codebreakers designed deciphering machines for each code version, which were constructed by NCR[63] in

---

[61] Where JN is short for Japanese and XX represents the version number. For example JN-19 stood for Japanese Naval Code version # 19.

[62] JN-39 and its successor JN-40 were codes used by Japanese merchant ships. The cracking of these codes provided the Allies with intelligence regarding the movements of Japanese merchant vessels and troop ships. By the end of war, American submarines, capitalizing on intelligence gleaned from JN-40, decimated the Japanese merchant fleet.

[63] NCR also built the 100 American Bombes used to crack the German U-Boat

Dayton, Ohio. Those involved in the construction soon realized that, at the core, all of these machines were utilizing the same electromechanical switching technology, custom-configured to address a specific requirement. What was needed was a universal machine that provided powerful base electric switching capability that could be quickly modified to address disparate requirements. Wasn't this what British and American bombe operators were doing when they "tuned" the bombes based on "menus" developed by codebreakers from cribs? Obviously, British codebreaker Tommy Flowers had been thinking along similar lines when he proposed a more efficient tube-based design that could be "programmed" via a series of switches and plugs to help crack the German Lorenz cipher.

This is the chain of events and line of reasoning that led the US military to develop a programmable computer.

The Battle of the Coral Sea

Flushed by their early success, the Japanese Army decided to extend their defensive ring southward by invading Port Moresby in New Guinea and Tulagi in the Solomon Islands chain. Air bases there would threaten Australia's supply lines and maybe even drive her out of the war.

In March 1942 British and American code-breakers intercepted JN25 radio traffic, alerting them to the Japanese plan. In mid-April British code-breakers in Ceylon[64] intercepted additional signals revealing that the Japanese carriers *Shokaku* and *Zuikaku* had been detached from Admiral Nagumo's Carrier Strike Force to support the

ciphers.
[64] Today's Sri Lanka.

landings. Under Admiral Ernest J. King's leadership, the American Navy, determined to hold the line in the Pacific until additional forces could be mobilized, ordered US carriers *Yorktown* and *Lexington* into the Coral Sea to oppose the offensive. A joint Australian-US cruiser force was dispatched to screen the carriers.

Beginning on 7 May the opposing carrier forces engaged in airstrikes over two consecutive days. The US sank a Japanese light carrier, *Shōhō*, and damaged *Shokaku*. The Japanese smashed the slow-moving *Lexington*, which was scuttled later to avoid capture, and damaged *Yorktown*. Having suffered losses to their respective air groups of over 55%, the two forces disengaged. Lacking sufficient air forces to cover their Port Moresby landing, the Japanese invasion fleet withdrew.

The Battle of the Coral Sea was significant for several reasons. It was the first time in history that a naval battle was fought without either surface fleet sighting the other. New technologies, specifically SIGINT, radar, and aviation, enabled the US to wage war more intelligently at greater distances. It also confirmed the value of British and American intelligence sharing per the informal agreement reached during the Atlantic Conference in Placentia Bay, Newfoundland, in August of 1941. The Coral Sea was where the Allies halted the Japanese advance.

Midway Island

Ten days after the Japanese attack on Pearl Harbor Chester W. Nimitz was named Commander-In-Chief of the United States Pacific Fleet. By the time he reached Hawaii and assumed command on December 31, there was general fear among Admiral Kimmel's existing staff that heads would roll. The attack on Pearl Harbor had left them shaken.

Some officers had turned prematurely gray. Others were taking sedatives to manage anxiety. But Nimitz wisely refused to cast blame.

Lt. Commander Edwin Layton, who had been Admiral Kimmel's chief intelligence officer believed Kimmel and General Short, Kimmel's US Army counterpart, were scapegoats for Washington's failures. Specifically, Layton blamed Admiral Richmond K. Turner for monopolizing intelligence that could have alerted Kimmel that Pearl Harbor was a potential Japanese target.

Nimitz's superior officer, Admiral King, Commander in Chief of the United States Fleet and Chief of Naval Operations during World War II, was a tough but fair man.[65] He was aware of the factionalism that contributed to the Pearl Harbor debacle and issued orders to centralize intelligence operations in Washington. Turner responded by relieving OP-20-G's commander, Captain Laurence Safford. Safford was a capable officer; under his watch, the Navy began building its worldwide naval collection and direction-finding capability. Safford also collaborated on the invention of the SIGABA.[66] Before his relief, Safford had assigned chief responsibility for cracking Japan's principal naval code to Hawaii's Station Hypo. To provide support, he had encouraged Lt. Commander Joesph Rochefort, Hypo's commanding officer, to cherry-pick the very best Navy cryptanalysts.

Rochefort and Layton were close friends who had studied Japanese together in Tokyo during the interwar years. Based on Station Hypo's progress in cracking JN-25

---

[65] FDR quipped that King was so tough, he shaved with a blowtorch.

[66] A cipher machine built and used by the United States for message encryption from World War II until the 1950s. There is no evidence that the security provided by SIGABA was ever compromised.

and the creative way they used traffic analysis, Rochefort convinced Layton that Midway, which the Japanese codenamed AF, was the next target. OP-20-G in Washington demurred. They believed AF could be one of several targets.[67] Nimitz was caught between them. To break the impasse, Station Hypo had Midway transmit a message "in the clear," reporting that Midway's saltwater condensers had broken down. A Japanese listening station intercepted the message and dutifully informed Tokyo that AF was having trouble with its saltwater condensers. The success of this "seeding operation," combined with the reliability of Rochefort and Layton's intelligence regarding Japanese intentions in the Coral Sea, convinced Nimitz. Nimitz pressed his case with King in Washington, and King gave way.

The American victory at Midway, where the US Navy sank all four of the Imperial Japanese Navy's heavy carriers and killed the cream of their naval airmen, for the loss of one Essex-class carrier,[68] was the turning point of the naval war in the Pacific. It was clear from the British raid on the Italian Fleet at Taranto, the Japanese attack on Pearl Harbor, the sinking of the *HMS Prince of Wales* and *Repulse*,[69] the battle of Coral Sea, and now Midway, that carriers, not battleships, would constitute the principal strike arm of the war in the Pacific.

Operation Vengeance

Operation Vengeance was the code name for the American plan to kill Admiral Isoroku Yamamoto, commander of the IJN. On April 18, 1943, Yamamoto and his

---

[67] Including Port Moresby, New Caledonia, Fiji, Hawaii or the US West Coast. Obviously, they had no idea.

[68] U.S.S. *Yorktown* (CV-5)

[69] Both sunk by Japanese aircraft on 10 December 1941.

staff planned to fly from Rabaul to Balalae Airfield, on an island near Bougainville, to inspect Japanese air units and boost morale following their defeat at Guadalcanal. The flight was scheduled to depart Rabaul at 06:00 and arrive at Balalae at 08:00, Tokyo time. Two medium bombers were assigned to transport the Admiral and his staff. Six navy fighters were detailed as escorts.

On April 14, the Admiral's itinerary was encoded using JN-25D and transmitted to affected units. The message was intercepted and decrypted by codebreakers at Station Hypo. The details were forwarded up the chain of command, and permission to "get Yamamoto" was granted. On April 18 Army P-38s from Kukum Field on Guadalcanal, maintaining radio silence and flying low over the ocean to evade Japanese radar, succeeded in ambushing the flight and shooting down the bombers. Admiral Yamamoto was killed in the attack. A cover story was circulated in the American press to hide codebreaking's role in the operation.

Operation Vengeance marked the first time that a "High-Value Individual (HVI)" or "Target of Opportunity" had been executed using airpower. Traditional political and military doctrine was to avoid intentionally killing High State officials and senior military officers because of the restraining influence they exercised on combatants. It was their responsibility to keep wars from descending into gratuitous butchery.[70]

Operation Vengeance foreshadowed modern HVI operations.[71] SIGINT was used to gather information about

---

[70] History is replete with examples. During the Pacific War, Japanese officers routinely refused surrender resulting in savage fighting that did nothing to alter the course of the war. The "Highway of Death" in the 1991 Gulf War provides another example. When US General Colin Powell was apprised of the killing taking place along Highway 80, he advised the President that the war was beginning to degrade into a pointless slaughter and therefore should be ended.

Yamamoto and determine his location. A joint task force was struck to plan the mission and assemble the equipment necessary to carry it out. The strike was conducted in enemy airspace. All preparations for the mission had to be compressed within the timeframe derived from the intelligence. Senior officials[72] sanctioned the mission, and the role played by intelligence operatives was kept secret by fabricating a cover story for the press.

The Boeing B-29

In the lead-up to World War II, the United States Army Air Corps (USAAF) determined that the B-17's range was not sufficient for operations in the Pacific. Therefore, in December 1939, they issued a formal specification for a new advanced bomber. Boeing submitted the winning design, which was designated XB-29. The B-29 was designed to achieve speeds exceeding 350 miles per hour, reach altitudes over 30,000 feet, and cover a range of approximately 4,000 miles.

Manufacturing the B-29 was a mammoth undertaking. It involved four main assembly factories: a pair of Boeing-operated plants at Renton, Washington, and Wichita, Kansas, a Bell plant at Marietta, Georgia, and a Martin plant at Omaha, Nebraska. Thousands of subcontractors were also involved in the project.

The combined effects of the aircraft's highly advanced design, challenging requirements, immense pressure for production, and hurried development caused many setbacks. The first B-29s rolled off the assembly line before

---

[71] Compare any modern day UAV or "drone" strike.

[72] Some historians believe that President Roosevelt made the decision to carry out Operation Vengeance but there is no evidence to support this. Certainly Admiral Nimitz knew about and approved of the plan.

being adequately tested. These early designs required so many upgrades that they were flown directly from the factory to ad hoc modification depots.

In August 1943, the Joint Chiefs, expecting victory in Europe[73], began planning for the buildup of forces in the East. President Roosevelt, fearing the repercussions if China was knocked out of the war before the Allies could fully mobilize against the Japanese, promised an air armada of 200 B-29s. But by the end of 1943 fewer than twenty of the one hundred aircraft delivered were operational. What followed has been dubbed the Battle of Kansas.

Under withering presidential pressure, Hap Arnold, chief of the USAAF,[74] flew to Kansas, where he autographed the one hundred and seventy-fifth B-29, demanding it be ready by March 1st, 1944.[75] The generals overseeing the project jumped, and by the 28th of February, the "HAP Arnold Special" and all of the B-29s ahead of it had rolled off the production line.

By August of that same year US forces secured the Mariana Island chain in a bloody campaign. Three islands; Guam, Saipan, and Tinian; were within B-29 range of Japan. Five bases with airstrips long enough to accommodate the superbombers were hurriedly constructed.[76]

---

[73] At the beginning of the war, the United States and Great Britain agreed on a "Germany First" strategy. They considered the Nazis to be the greater threat, so defeating them was the top priority. After that, the Allies would concentrate on defeating Japan.

[74] Arnold suffered four heart attacks during the second half of WWII.

[75] The Hap Arnold Special made an emergency landing in the USSR, where it was impounded by the Soviets and reverse-engineered as the Soviet Tu-4.

[76] The foremen who oversaw construction of the runways questioned the USAAF's requirement for extra-long runways as it pushed back completion dates. In 1944, most of the information about the new superbomber was still classified.

On October the 12th, 1944, the first B-29 landed on Isley Air Field, Saipan, piloted by Brigadier General Heywood Hansell, 21st Bomber Command's commanding officer. Hansell was a planner and a staunch believer in strategic, high-altitude, precision bombardment. However, his theories failed to produce results. The B-29's engines were plagued with issues, exacerbated by 3,000-mile raids and the long climb to its 30,000-foot bombing altitude. The jet stream,[77] a previously unknown phenomenon, made accurate bombing next to impossible. Arnold relieved Hansell and replaced him with Curtis E. LeMay.

In contrast to Hansell, LeMay was an operator. After observing the results of the first few raids, LeMay saw no reason the 29 failed to perform apart from the way it was being used. Determined to get results, he stripped the plane of its defensive elements, including its gunners, and switched to night bombing at altitudes between five and 8,000 feet. This, he reasoned, would take the strain off the engines as they would no longer need to climb to 30,000 feet. When US aircrews protested that flying at such low altitudes without gunners was suicide, LeMay countered that the Japanese possessed limited radar and almost no night-fighting capability.

On the night of March 9-10, 1945, 330 B-29s launched a devastating attack on Tokyo. Employing a lethal cocktail of conventional bombs and incendiaries, the raid produced a firestorm that killed 100,000 Japanese, left another million homeless, and burned out approximately sixteen square miles of the downtown. More than sixty Japanese cities would receive the "LeMay treatment" over the next three months.

---

[77] The jet stream is a fast, narrow current of air flowing from west to east that encircles the globe.

On August 6 a B-29 dropped the first atomic bomb on Hiroshima, incinerating 78,000 inhabitants. When the Japanese failed to surrender, a second bomb was dropped on Nagasaki three days later. This attack, which demonstrated that the Americans had more bombs, combined with the rapid advance of Soviet forces in northeastern China, forced the Japanese to surrender.

The three billion dollars[78] spent on the design and production of B-29s made it the most expensive program of the war, far exceeding the $1.9 billion spent on the Manhattan Project.[79] In the summer of 1945, the four runways at North Field on Tinian comprised the largest airport in the world. The B-29's legacy was a lasting one. It laid the groundwork for all future strategic aircraft in the US Air Force inventory. After the war, B-29s were adapted for several functions, including in-flight refueling, parasite tests,[80] antisubmarine patrol, weather reconnaissance, and rescue duty.

Defining the Threat

The B-29 program confirmed the dire predictions of Douhet and Mitchell. Waging modern war required human and material resources on a scale that blurred the lines between soldiers and civilians. America had entered WWII advocating the doctrine of daylight strategic bombing, where precision raids would avoid civilian casualties while targeting assets vital to the German war machine such as factories, naval bases, shipyards, railroad yards, power plants, steel mills, and airfields. The firebombing of Japanese

---

[78] Over $40 billion in today's dollars at the time this book was written.
[79] The codename for the project to build atomic weapons.
[80] B-29s were used to carry "parasite aircraft" aloft for air launching such as the Bell X-1 that broke the sound barrier.

cities and atomic attacks on Hiroshima and Nagasaki, combined with the intentional obliteration of German cities by British Bomber Command and the USSAF at war's end, swept away the theoretical chalk line between combatants and non-combatants, and made civilians legitimate targets.

The Manhattan Project

Shortly before the outbreak of the war in Europe, German chemists Otto Hahn and Fritz Strassmann discovered nuclear fission. Their research fueled fears among Jewish scientists who had fled Europe due to German persecution that the Nazis might develop an atomic bomb. In August 1939 Hungarian-born physicists Leo Szilard and Eugene Wigner drafted a letter, signed by Einstein, apprising President Roosevelt of this threat.

The President convened a senior advisory group to study the issue. They recommended the US establish a nuclear research and development program. Colonel Leslie Groves, who had directed the Pentagon's construction, was appointed to oversee the project. Groves selected Robert Oppenheimer, a brilliant nuclear physicist from the University of Chicago, to head the team that would design the bomb. Since Army convention dictated that projects be codenamed after the district where they were located, the project was designated Manhattan.

The Manhattan Project was the second most expensive weapons program undertaken by the United States during World War II.[81] Research and production occurred at more than thirty facilities in the US, Britain, and

---

[81] The Manhattan Project cost more than $2 Billion dollars. Over 90% was spent on building plants to produce fissionable materials. Less than 10% was allocated for development and production of bombs.

Canada. In just two short years, the US Army Corps of Engineers built an industrial complex that rivaled the American automotive industry.

Most of the work was focused on constructing the three facilities that produced fissionable material.

The first was the electromagnetic isotope separation plant at Oak Ridge, Tennessee, code-named Y-12. The plant used calutrons to separate Uranium 235 from Uranium 238. The calutrons were configured in a race track layout. A magnetic field passed throughout the oval of calutrons, causing the divergence of streams of U235 and U238 so that the separated isotopes could be collected. A single calutron captured a mere 10 grams of U235 daily.[82] One thousand one hundred fifty-two calutrons were built by war's end.

The second facility was the Hanford Engineer Works in Hanford, Washington, code-named "Site W". In 1941 scientists discovered that plutonium, a man-made fuel, was nearly twice as likely to undergo fission as U235 and that it could be produced in large quantities by irradiating uranium in nuclear reactors. Three production reactors were constructed at Hanford.

The third facility was the gaseous diffusion plant at Oak Ridge, Tennessee, code-named K-25. K-25 was a massive facility that processed slightly enriched material from the S-50 thermal diffusion plant. This material was then fed into K-25, which, in turn, supplied its output to the Y-12 electromagnetic plant. Enclosing over two million square feet, K-25 was the largest structure built up to that time.

More than 600,000 civilians contributed to Manhattan by war's end. Operations at Oak Ridge consumed one-tenth of all the electrical power generated in the United States.

---

[82] It wasn't efficient, but it worked.

With a population of 75,000, Oak Ridge became Tennessee's fifth-largest town.

By the spring of 1945, Oppenheimer and his Los Alamos scientists were ready to test "the gadget". On May 7, 1945, a pre-test explosion using ninety tons of TNT was conducted to calibrate the instruments used to measure the bomb's impact. On July 16, 1945, the first atomic bomb exploded with an energy equivalent to twenty kilotons of TNT, beating scientists' estimates. The shockwave was felt one hundred miles away, and the mushroom cloud ascended to 35,000 feet.

President Truman was attending an Allied conference at Potsdam when he received news that the bomb had been successfully tested. To avoid invading the Japanese home islands, Truman and his administration decided to drop the atomic bomb on Japan.

On August 6, 1945, the Enola Gay[83], a specially modified B-29 piloted by Paul Tibbets, took off from North Field on Tinian. The mission went as planned; the bomb was dropped on the primary target, Hiroshima. Approximately 80,000 people were killed, and another 70,000 injured. When the Japanese had still not surrendered three days later, a second bomb was dropped on Nagasaki. Kokura had been the primary target for this raid, but it was clouded over, so the plane proceeded to its secondary. These bombings, combined with the lightening Soviet invasion of Northeastern China, brought the Second World War to an end.

---

[83] Enola Gay was the maiden name of Tibbet's mother.

Operation Paperclip – *"Mein Führer! I can walk!"* - Dr. Strangelove (1964)

Before the Allies stormed the beaches of Normandy, a joint British-American task force, codenamed Operation Overcast, was struck to comb Europe for valuable German military, scientific, and technological research. The original plan was to use German technology to help win the war against Japan. However, the operation was quickly transformed into a permanent immigration program once senior officials realized that the German scientists behind this research were essential for transferring the technology—a process now known in the technology industry as "knowledge transfer." The revised program was named Operation Paperclip after the paperclips officials attached to the folders of the Germans selected for emigration.

Paperclip cast a wide net; top scientists involved in aviation, rocket design, synthetics, medicine, chemical and biological weapons, and wireless communications were the most sought-after assets. As the Cold War progressed, former German Intelligence Officers were added to the program. By the time Paperclip ended in 1959, more than 1,600 German subject matter experts with their 4,400 dependants had been relocated to the United States for employment in Government-sponsored agencies.

The US and British governments made every effort to keep the details of Operation Paperclip secret because nearly half of the Germans transferred under the program were former Nazi Party members. President Truman explicitly directed that ex-Nazis be excluded from the program. However, the officials in charge of the selections, recognizing the best candidates were former party members, redacted the files to ensure approval. As the Cold War escalated and Americans saw the Soviet Union as a significant threat to US security, integrating "ex-Nazi" scientists into the program was deemed preferable to leaving them to the Soviets.

The influx of so many top German scientists was a windfall for the American Defense Department: the US had already assembled the world's leading physicists to develop nuclear weapons, and now they had the men who could build the rockets to deliver the bombs to their targets.

Post-War Europe

By mid-1947 the ideological differences the Allies had papered over to defeat Nazi Germany resurfaced. The Americans and British wanted a free Europe established on democratic principles. The USSR had suffered twenty million casualties during the war—twenty times the combined losses of Britain and the U.S. Their main objective was to bring countries occupied by Soviet troops into their sphere of influence, establishing a buffer zone of satellite states along their western border.

Unable to win a conventional war and unwilling to use nuclear weapons unless confronted by a direct threat—a situation the USSR, who did not yet possess nuclear weapons, was careful to avoid— the Americans took two decisions: to reduce communism's appeal by establishing a prosperous post-war economy where non-communist nations would have unfettered access to raw materials and global markets, and to reorganize US forces into an integrated security apparatus capable of detecting and countering the Soviet threat. To kick-start the economic recovery, the United States introduced the Marshall Plan. To lay the groundwork for its new security apparatus, the Truman administration signed the National Security Act into law on July 26, 1947.

As outlined by Congress in the preamble, the purpose of the National Security Act was to establish a Department of Defense, encompassing the Army, Navy, and Air Force under the direction of the Secretary of Defense, to provide for their unified direction, and to eliminate unnecessary duplication particularly in the field of research and engineering.

The Act also created the National Security Council, the Central Intelligence Agency (CIA), and the National Security Agency (NSA).

The Cold War

The Cold War began in earnest on August 29, 1949, when the Soviet Union detonated its first atomic bomb, dubbed "Joe 1" by US intelligence operatives. Emboldened by his new weapon and Mao Zedong's declaration of a communist China, Stalin reversed his previous decision and gave Kim Il Sung permission to invade South Korea using Soviet-supplied artillery and armor. Labeled a police action by Harry Truman, who viewed the conflict as one between United Nations forces and North Korean aggressors backed by Soviet and Chinese communists, the battle lines rolled back and forth for a year before settling down into a bloody stalemate. After exhaustive negotiations, the war terminated in an armistice on 27 July 1953.

For the US and her Allies, the Korean War confirmed that the communists were prepared to use force to expand their influence beyond their existing borders. As President Truman stated during a televised address to the American people on June 25, 1950: "This attack has made it clear, beyond all doubt, that the international communist movement is willing to use armed invasion to conquer independent nations."

Truman's decision to develop thermonuclear weapons, taken just one month after the USSR detonated her first atomic device, had been a controversial one. The invasion of South Korea by Soviet-backed forces galvanized American opinion. The Soviets had the bomb and they had already produced copies of the B-29 flying fortress to deliver it. Moving forward, America would step up her defense efforts.

"In a Nuclear War, Surprise Means Annihilation." **- US Secretary of Defense, Robert McNamara**

In 1944 Vice President Truman was advocating for the creation of a unified security apparatus. He believed that America's failure to prevent the Japanese attack on Pearl Harbor was due to the fragmented nature of US intelligence operations. When Truman became President, he was determined to ensure that America was never caught off guard again.

Understanding the effect Japan's attack on Pearl Harbor had on the American psyche is critical to understanding post-war America. America is unique among nations because she possesses all the resources necessary to survive and thrive without relying on imports. Separated from Europe and Asia by vast oceans, she is a self-sufficient fortress that, for centuries, was insulated from the wars of the other great powers. Being attacked on her native soil, even if it was on the faraway island of Hawaii, shocked Americans.

This is why the Truman administration created the kind of security apparatus it did. In 1947 the US was the only nation armed with nuclear weapons. She could have imposed her will on the USSR if she chose to do so. Instead, she changed the name of the War Department to the

Department of Defense. The primary purpose of the NSA and the CIA is to detect foreign threats. It is a defensive, not offensive, posture. Unlike the Great Powers that preceded her, the US did not need "Lebensraum;"[84] she was focused on exploiting the land and resources within her own country. Living peacefully within her borders, Americans could not understand why the Soviets were so obsessed with theirs.

In contrast, The Soviets lumped the Americans in with the "Imperialist" powers who had invaded Russia, starting with Napoleon in 1812. Neither side empathized with the other, which made the Cold War all the more dangerous.

Funding the Military

When the Korean War started in 1950, US defense spending totaled $13.7 billion. When it ended, three years later, this figure had quadrupled. Before Korea, American defense spending decreased significantly between wars. A nuclear-armed USSR and China's incursion in Korea changed that.[85] For the next decade, American defense spending remained at wartime levels. Currently, the United States spends more on defense than the next nine countries combined.

Most countries, including the United States, introduced or increased income taxes to fund their participation in the Great War. In the U.S., income tax accounted for about five percent of GDP. After the war, income taxes dropped to two and a half percent, with the expectation that they would be further reduced or, in some countries—such as Canada, which introduced income tax as

---

[84] Territory believed by Nazis to be necessary for economic self-sufficiency.
[85] Aggressors never seem to learn that provocations are counterproductive. They only compel potential adversaries to strengthen their defenses.

a temporary measure—discontinued once the war debt was discharged.

During WWII, The Roosevelt administration hiked personal income taxes to fifteen percent of US GDP, a rate which has continued down to the present day. To raise additional funds, the government issued war bonds that post-war inflation made easier to pay back. During the Korean War, there was little appetite for war bonds. To cover the shortfall, the United States began issuing long-term Treasuries. The seductive appeal of "passing the buck" by buying now and leaving the next administration to pay later achieved its purpose. The US acquired the funds necessary to construct the post-war security complex it envisioned, but the price was a dramatic increase in the national debt. Ironically, at the time of this writing, debt poses the greatest threat to the global economy and by extension, US national security.

Military Research

During the 1940s the United States built a vast network of military research and production facilities to develop the technologies used to defeat the Axis powers. Truman's post-war decision to develop a thermonuclear device, combined with a top-secret National Security Council paper recommending a massive military buildup and "an accelerated exploitation of US scientific potential" to address the emerging Soviet threat, fueled further expansion.

Developing the technologies necessary to fight a thermonuclear war was not going to be accomplished by gifted amateurs such as Morse and Bell tinkering in their basements. It required the expertise of the world's brightest scientists, working within a vast network of cutting-edge laboratories directed by the Defense Department and the

CIA and supported by the world's largest economy. Alvin Weinberg, an American nuclear physicist and Director of Oak Ridge National Laboratory during the Manhattan Project, termed this immense scientific endeavor "Big Science."

The Key Laboratories – "...*war is too important to be left to politicians.*" Dr. Strangelove (1964)

The foundation for "Big Science" was laid by President Truman's predecessor, Franklin D. Roosevelt. Six months before America entered the war in December 1941, Roosevelt created The Office of Scientific Research and Development (OSRD). Headed by chief scientist Vannevar Bush, its mission was to coordinate scientific research for military purposes during World War II. Provided with nearly unlimited funding and resources, the OSRD directed projects such as developing the proximity fuse, producing penicillin at scale, enhancing radar, and the Manhattan Project.

Under Bush's administration, the OSRD oversaw the creation and or direction of the following research facilities:

• The Lawrence Berkeley National Laboratory at the University of California's Berkeley campus. The facility was named for Ernest O. Lawrence, inventor of the cyclotron and winner of the 1939 Nobel Prize in Physics. During the Manhattan Project, research conducted at this facility determined that plutonium 239 was 1.7 times more likely to fission than uranium 235.

• The now famous Los Alamos National Laboratory, also known as Project Y, was constructed in Los Alamos, New Mexico, to design and build an atomic bomb.

• Clinton National Laboratories in Oak Ridge, Tennessee. Code-named X-10; it was operated by the

University of Chicago Metallurgical Laboratory. Constructed by the US Government in 1943, it was renamed The Oak Ridge National Laboratory in 1948. Its initial purpose was to provide the Manhattan Project with a pilot plant to produce trace plutonium. The large plutonium-production reactors and chemical facilities built later in Hanford, Washington - a location selected because of its remoteness and abundance of water to cool the reactors, provided the bulk plutonium needed for the bombs.

• In 1942 a team of physicists constructed Chicago Pile-1 in the squash court under the west stands of Stagg Field at the University of Chicago. Pile-1 was the site of the world's first controlled, self-sustaining nuclear reaction. Because the experiments were deemed too dangerous to conduct in a major city, operations were moved to nearby Palos Hills, where a new facility was constructed. It was named The Argonne National Laboratory after the surrounding Argonne Forest.

• The Ames Laboratory, affiliated with Iowa State University, in Ames, Iowa. In 1942 Ames scientists developed a process for producing nearly pure uranium, making it possible to cast large uranium ingots for nuclear reactors. The Ames Project produced more than 2 million pounds of uranium for the Manhattan Project.

• Knolls Atomic Power Laboratory is located in Niskayuna, New York. Initially run by G.E., the laboratory was responsible for researching, designing, constructing, operating, and maintaining US nuclear-powered warships. Its current mandate is to explore atomic energy for defense and power generation.

After the war, General Leslie Groves was commissioned to build three additional laboratories:

- The Sandia National Laboratories at Kirkland Air Force Base in Albuquerque, New Mexico. The laboratory began in 1945 as Z Division, the ordnance design, testing, and assembly arm of Los Alamos National Laboratory. Its primary purpose was to engineer and manufacture deliverable nuclear weapons designed by Los Alamos. The first atomic bombs, Little Boy and Fat Man, were one-off designs. Sandia introduced the necessary standardization, assembly line production, and quality control to manufacture America's arsenal of tactical and strategic bombs.

- The Brookhaven National Laboratory is in Upton, New York, on the former US Army Camp Upton site. It was constructed in 1947 primarily as a nuclear research facility.

- The Livermore Laboratory was established in 1952 to spur innovation and provide competition to the nuclear weapon design laboratory at Los Alamos. The name was later expanded to the Lawrence Livermore National Laboratory in recognition of the contributions of Ernest Lawrence, the former director of the Radiation Laboratory at Berkeley from which the laboratory evolved. Livermore's first director, Herb York, would become the first chief scientist of the Advanced Research Projects Agency (ARPA) in 1958.

The Birth of the Computer Era

The electronic computer was the defining technology that propelled the world from the industrial age into the information technology era.

In the 1930s a computer was someone who sat at a desk with pad and pencil performing numerical computations. In some cases, mechanical tabulating devices were also used. Imagine an old model typewriter. You press down a key, which, in turn, moves a lever with steel type to hit a ribbon and transfer ink to paper. It is a "mechanical" process. Early tabulating devices functioned the same way.

When the European war broke out in 1939, the US began ramping up her military preparedness. Her outdated forces required advanced equipment, such as radios, heavy bombers, single-engine monoplane fighters, modern artillery pieces, radar, sonar, and underwater mines. Understanding the capabilities and limitations of these technologies was crucial to effectively utilizing them in combat.

For example, what should the barrel's elevation be if an artillery officer needs to put a shell on a target five miles downrange? What if it is five and one-half miles—or six? Different artillery pieces also have different calibers. How does this impact the calculations?

In the field, artillery officers don't have time for calculations or errors that could lead to a "short round," particularly when firing over the heads of their own troops. Instead, they consult the manual that came with the weapon. They run their finger down the page to the row that marks the distance they want the shell to travel and then across the page to the column that tells them the angle of the barrel. This is called a ballistics table. Compiling these tables took hundreds of computer hours, and hundreds more to check each calculation.

Now, imagine you want to sew the entrance to an enemy harbor with magnetic mines. How close would you need to space them in order to obtain maximum coverage? The answer depends on a number of factors, such as the explosive force of the mine, the power of the magnet, and the strength of the current. There are also many different types of mines. Again, making these calculations required hundreds of computer hours.

Now, what if you could speed up the process? What if you had a machine that could calculate 100 times faster than a human computer—or a thousand human computers?

This requirement is what prompted the U.S. War Department to invest in computer research. This is also why the first machines were called computers. Moving forward, a mechanical computer would do the computing. A "programmer" would write instructions detailing the required calculations and the order in which they were to be performed, and a computer technician or "tech" would configure the computer's settings to execute the program.

The Harvard Mark 1 – *"It sounded like a thousand knitting needles." - Rear Admiral Grace Hopper*

The Harvard Mark 1 was an electromechanical computer[86] designed by Howard Aiken, an applied mathematics instructor at Harvard University. Built by IBM at their Endicott, N.Y. facility, the Mark 1 incorporated existing telegraph, telephone, and business machine technologies. The Harvard Mark 1 was eight feet tall, fifty-one feet long, and two feet thick. It weighed five tons, had 3,500 multipole relays, and contained 500 miles of wire. It used three paper-tape readers, two card readers, a card punch, and two typewriters for input and output.

Crude by today's standards, the Harvard Mark 1 was America's first automatic digital computing machine and the largest electromechanical device ever constructed. Its calculations were based on the decimal system.[87]

---

[86] It had mechanical switches that opened and closed.
[87] The Harvard Mark 1 introduced the term "bug" to computing when operators found an actual moth causing malfunctions, leading to the now-familiar phrase

Delivered to Harvard in 1944, the Mark 1 cost $500,000 to build, $300,000 of which came from IBM. The remaining $200,000 was provided by the US Navy, which commandeered the machine until war's end in 1945.

The Navy's Bureau of Ships used the Mark 1 to perform calculations to protect ships from magnetic mines and to design radar transmitters. John von Neumann, a brilliant scientist and mathematician involved with the Manhattan Project, used it to determine the best method for inducing a nuclear reaction: the implosion method, which compresses a sphere of fissile material with explosives, or the gun design method, where one sub-critical mass is fired into another.[88]

ENIAC

In contrast to the Harvard Mark 1, which relied on electromagnetic switches, the Electronic Numerical Integrator and Computer (ENIAC)[89] used electronic valves (vacuum tubes) for calculating. Because vacuum tubes have no moving parts, ENIAC was several orders of magnitude faster than its electromechanical predecessor.

Conceived and designed by Presper Eckert and John Mauchly of the University of Pennsylvania, Moore School of Electrical Engineering, ENIAC was financed by the United States Army, Ordnance Corps, Research and Development Command to calculate artillery firing tables for the Army's Ballistic Research Laboratory.

---

for technical glitches.

[88] The implosion method proved to be the most practicable method.

[89] ""And 'Computer' was added by a prescient Army procurement officer who recognized ENIAC's flexibility and aimed to structure the contract to accommodate future uses beyond those specified in the original solicitation. This approach avoided the need for drafting a new contract each time the machine was upgraded for a new project."

The contract was signed on June 5, 1943, and construction began the following month under the codename Project PX. The US Army Ordnance Corps formally accepted ENIAC in July 1946. The original contract was $61,700, but due to cost overruns, the final cost was almost $500,000. In 1947 ENIAC was moved to the US Army's Aberdeen Proving Ground in Maryland where it remained in continuous operation until powered down in 1955.

ENIAC was the first programmable electronic digital computer. It used conditional branching, which means it could take different actions depending on the product of a previous calculation. Conditional branching enabled ENIAC to perform a wider range of tasks more efficiently, streamlining the programming process and enhancing overall productivity. While ENIAC was initially designed to calculate artillery range tables, its first project focused on calculating the dynamics of thermonuclear explosions and other aspects critical to the design and construction of thermonuclear weapons.

ENIAC was a truly massive machine. It was over a hundred feet long, eight feet tall, three feet wide, and weighed thirty tons. It filled a 1,500-square-foot room and consumed 150 KW of electricity. Because ENIAC's 17,000 vacuum tubes generated large amounts of heat, the room was equipped with air conditioning.

ENIAC incorporated many modern computer technology concepts and principles in its design and introduced descriptors such as runtime, downtime, and programming. It also propagated misconceptions that remained long after technological advancements eliminated them. For example, during the 1980s, many users believed it was detrimental to switch off their machines—a throwback to ENIAC when powering it up and down caused its tubes to fail, an issue that was obviated when transistors replaced tubes.

Distribution of Early Computers

Even before ENIAC became operational, Mauchly, Eckert, and Arthur Burks—another engineer from the Moore School of Electrical Engineering at the University of Pennsylvania—began designing a more advanced machine: the Electronic Discrete Variable Automatic Computer (EDVAC), which would incorporate stored programming and significantly improve computational efficiency. John Von Neumann joined the group and kept notes on the proceedings. Herman Goldstine, an officer appointed by the Army to act as liaison between its Ballistic Research Laboratory (BRL) at Aberdeen Proving Ground and the University, typed up these notes and distributed them widely.

Goldstine was one of a new breed of liaison officers who understood both the needs of the military and the technologies available to meet them. As the number of technologies has expanded, so too have the contractors who navigate seamlessly between the private and public sectors, blurring the lines between them. Today it's common for security agents with a top-secret clearance to be on payrolls of private companies where they are outsourced to governmental and non-governmental agencies and corporations.

After the war, Goldstine teamed up with von Neumann and Burks at the Institute for Advanced Study at Princeton, where they constructed an Immediate Access Store (IAS) machine. In contrast to ENIAC, which required manual adjustments of switches and cables for each operation, IAS machines incorporated a memory system that stored both instructions and data. This capability to store instructions allowed IAS machines to perform a broader range of functions without the need for manual reconfiguration. The IAS machine produced about a dozen direct descendants. The first to operate was at the Argonne National Laboratory at Oak Ridge; AVIDAC, which began operations in 1953. The University of Illinois built ORDVAC for the Ballistic Research Laboratory at Aberdeen Proving Ground and a twin version called ILLIAC for themselves. SILLIAC, CSIRAC, WISC, Cyclone, MISTIC, George, and computers at Iowa State and Michigan State were created in ILLIAC's image. The RAND Corporation built JOHNIAC in honor of John von Neumann to test transistor logic. MANIAC I, the Los Alamos version of the IAS, became operational in early 1952.

IBM's 701 was also based on the IAS design, becoming the forerunner of a whole series of machines that went on to dominate the commercial computer market. As per the table below, the first computers went almost exclusively to the defense establishment, military contractors, and private universities conducting defense research.

Buyer	Government	Military Contractor	University	Business
IBM World Headquarters, New York, N.Y. (1952)		X		
University of California, Los Alamos, N.M. (1953)			X	
Lockheed Aircraft Company, Glendale, Cal. (1953)		X		
National Security Agency, Washington, D.C. (1953)	X			

Buyer	Government	Military Contractor	University	Business
Douglas Aircraft Company, Santa Monica, Cal. (1953)		X		
General Electric Company., Lockland, Ohio (1953)[90]		X		
Convair, Fort Worth, Tex. (1953)		X		
US Navy, Inyokern, Cal. (1953)	X			
United Aircraft, East Hartford, Conn. (1953)		X		
North American Aviation, Santa Monica, Cal. (1953)		X		
Rand Corporation., Santa Monica, Cal. (1953)		X		
Boeing Corporation, Seattle, Wash. (1953)		X		
Douglas Aircraft Company, El Segundo, Cal. (1954)		X		
Naval Aviation Supply, Philadelphia, Pa. (1954)		X		
University of California, Livermore, Cal. (1954)			X	
General Motors Corporation, Detroit, Mich. (1954)			X	
Lockheed Aircraft Company, Glendale, Cal. (1954)		X		X
US Weather Bureau, Washington, D.C.	X			

---

[90] GE was tapped by the Truman Administration to bring quality control and mass production standards to the assembly of the country's stockpile of nuclear warheads.

Buyer	Government	Military Contractor	University	Business
(1955)				
Dupont Central Research, Wilmington, DE (1954)		X		

EDVAC spawned the UNIVAC 1, America's first successful commercial computer. Again, like the IBM 701, the first UNIVAC machines went almost exclusively to defense, military contractors, and private universities that conducted defense research.

Buyer	Government	Military Contractor	University	Business
Bureau of the Census, Commerce Dept., Suitland, Maryland	X			
Office of the Air Comptroller, USAF, Washington, D.C.	X			
Army Map Service, US Army, Washington, D.C.	X			
New York University (for Atomic Energy Commission), NY, NY			X	
University of Cal., Radiation Laboratory, Livermore, California			X	
David Taylor Model Basin, U.S.N. Bureau of Ships, Maryland	X			
Prudential Insurance Company				X
General Electric Company[91]		X		

Clearly, it was the needs of the Defense department and Defense spending that drove the development of early computers.

The installation of computers at US universities gave the military access to extended research facilities and America's brightest young minds. In turn, the universities produced computer scientists and programmers to staff the National Labs and build new weapons systems. During the 1950s, the Department of Defense provided 70% of all research funding to US universities.

Thermonuclear Weapons - *"Gee, I wish we had one of them doomsday machines." -* Dr. Strangelove (1964)

In November 1952 the United States successfully detonated her first multi-megaton thermonuclear device at Eniwetok Atoll in the Pacific Proving Ground in the Marshall Islands. The USSR countered nine months later detonating her first thermonuclear bomb at the Semipalatinsk test site in northern Kazakhstan.

"Our Germans are better than their Germans." The Right Stuff (1983)

To deliver thermonuclear weapons, both the US and USSR engaged in crash programs to develop intercontinental ballistic missiles powered by liquid fuel engines. The Soviets had conducted their own post-war Operation Paperclip in which they abducted approximately 2,000 German rocket scientists and spirited them back to the USSR. To counter the

---

[91] During and after the war, General Electric (GE) played an important role in nuclear research & weapons manufacturing, the development of radar, and the design and construction of jet engines.

US bomber threat, the Soviets also stepped up development of long-range bombers.

Both sides spent enormous treasure on these programs. For the US, far and away the world's largest post war economy — half of all manufactured goods were made in the U.S.A.— the price was paid with a steady rise in inflation and personal income tax. In the Soviet Union, people did without.

"No Bucks, No Buck Rogers." - The Right Stuff (1983)

Eisenhower's top priority upon taking office in January 1953 was to end the Korean War and bring the troops home. His second was to get spending under control. This necessitated focusing on defense, where his administration expended the most funds. However, the Republicans were divided on defense spending. Senate majority leader Robert Taft wanted to slash the budget and provide tax cuts to Americans, believing this was the only way the GOP could gain control of the House of Representatives in the next election. Senator McCarthy and his supporters argued that advocating for defense cuts equated to supporting communists.

At the same time, America's Strategic Air Command (SAC) was clamoring for additional information about the USSR. How could Air Force colonels create comprehensive strike packages without knowing the precise locations of Soviet bases, their key industries, how well they were defended, or the terrain the bomber crews would encounter on their way to and from their targets?

As President, Eisenhower had to balance all these interests, spending what was necessary but no more. Since informed defense cuts could not be made without reliable assessments of Soviet capabilities, Eisenhower's most pressing intelligence priority was to ascertain the true extent of the Soviet threat.

As early as 1945 the Truman administration had attempted to establish a network of European intelligence operatives, led by Alan Dulles and Richard Helms of the Office of Strategic Services (OSS), to gather intelligence from inside the Soviet Union. However, the KGB quickly rounded up the agents, and they were summarily shot or imprisoned in the gulags. Unbeknownst to the CIA, agency security had been compromised by Soviet master spy Kim Philby who, as the head of British intelligence in Washington, was read into every covert operation the US conducted in Europe.

Multiple attempts were also made to document Russian radar and electronic communications frequencies by flying near and inside Soviet airspace. This was dangerous work and several US aircraft were damaged or shot down. Unmanned spy balloons equipped with electronic devices to collect data on Soviet weather patterns for SAC were tried as well, but most were either unrecoverable or destroyed by MiG-15s.[92]

Eisenhower convoked a task group in 1953 to find solutions. The following year the committee submitted a report recommending initiating a spy satellite program. One of the burning questions the delegates debated was whether orbiting a satellite over the USSR would violate Soviet airspace. At the time, there was no established precedent stipulating the altitude of a nation's protected airspace. More troubling for the President, satellite technology would not be practicable for several years and he needed solutions now.

---

[92] The Mikoyan-Gurevich MiG-15 is a jet fighter aircraft developed by Mikoyan-Gurevich for the Soviet Union. The MiG-15 was one of the first successful jet fighters to incorporate swept wings to achieve high transonic speeds.

The U-2 - *"Smile, you're on Candid Camera!"* (1960)

In 1954 Edwin Land, who was serving as a technical advisor to the President, proposed a stop-gap solution. Land's company, Polaroid, had supplied the Allies with anti-glare goggles, gun sights, viewfinders, cameras, stereoscopic glasses, and other optical devices with polarizing lenses during WWII. Drawing on his experience with stereoscopic lenses, which were used to visualize geographic features captured in reconnaissance photographs in three dimensions, Land believed that specially designed cameras and lenses could be created sufficient to capture high-resolution images of the USSR from very high altitudes. But at what altitude? How high would an airplane need to fly to evade Soviet MiGs and surface-to-air missiles?

The USAF knew from flight testing the MiG-15, provided by Lt. No Kum-Sok of the North Korean Air Force when he defected in 1953 that its service ceiling was just under 50,000 feet. They also knew the maximum range of the Soviet early warning radar was 65,000 feet because the US had supplied the USSR with their radar sets during WWII via Lend-Lease. Therefore, as long as US pilots maintain altitudes above 65,000 feet, they should be safe.

With the specifications defined, questions remained about who would be responsible for procuring and maintaining a suitable aircraft and who would supply the pilots? Overflying Soviet airspace without permission was a violation of international law; doing it in a USAF plane could be construed as an act of war.

Consequently, Eisenhower appointed CIA Director Alan Dulles to run the program. Dulles tapped Dick Bissell to oversee the arrangements. Under "Mr. B's" direction, Kelly Johnson, President of Lockheed Martin's Skunkworks, would design and build the aircraft. Lockheed Martin would also supply the ground crews to maintain it. The Air Force would recruit the pilots, provide mission and weather planning, and run the airbases. To maintain secrecy, the pilots were put on Lockheed's payroll. James Baker of Harvard and Richard Scott Perkin of the Perkin-Elmer Company would design the specialized camera and lenses. The 5,400 feet of large-format film required for each mission (1,800 per camera), and post-flight processing, would be provided by Kodak.

Flying at 70,000 feet also required special fuel. The CIA contacted Jimmy Doolittle who had been recalled by the USAAF prior to WWII to develop 100-octane aircraft fuel. He convinced his connections at Shell to invest in the project.

Finally, the whole operation was funded by a secret CIA slush fund. There were no government markings on the aircraft or its design drawings, and the CIA procured a secluded property (Area 51)[93] in Nevada for testing.

The details of how the U-2 was developed still make for a gripping read, but what makes it pertinent to our story is how military expediency dictated next-generation technological development.

Every pound of weight added to the U-2 reduced its altitude by one foot. Ejection seats would have added 30 pounds above a regular seat, so they were left out.[94] There was constant bickering over the size of the camera. Unable to comprehend Johnson's intransigence, its designers threw up their hands in despair. "All we need is one more inch!" they complained. To which a red-faced Johnson snapped, "I would sell my grandmother for another inch!"

---

[93] Area 51 became the Defense Department's secret test base for experimental aircraft, which explains why so many sightings of unidentified flying objects occur in the area.

[94] This policy was overturned soon after pilots commenced test flights.

In the 1950s, computers were a hundred feet long and weighed thirty tons. Considering the challenge of integrating their processing capabilities into airplanes and satellites, it's clear why funding research to miniaturize components - to where they now fit in today's mobile devices - was a military priority.

Sputnik - *"I will not go to bed at night by the light of a Communist moon." -* Lyndon B. Johnson

Contrary to popular belief, Sputnik's launch did not catch the Eisenhower administration by surprise. Based on reconnaissance photos from a U-2 spy plane, the CIA had warned the President several months in advance about Soviet preparations for a launch. However, because U-2 intelligence was classified, the President could not defend himself against critics who accused the administration of being unprepared.

Actually, the US could have launched a satellite a full year before the Soviets. But launch preparations got bogged down in politics. In the 1950s, America's most advanced missile base was the Army's Redstone Arsenal in Huntsville, Alabama, which was led by German rocket scientists brought to the U.S. under Operation Paperclip. Competition to launch the first satellite came from Vanguard, a quasi-civilian (US Navy-funded) group of scientists. Ultimately, the government chose Vanguard over the Redstone scientists, even though Vanguard technology was unproven, because they wanted to put a scientific face on the mission. Nothing conveys hostility quite like using ex-Nazis to launch rockets designed to carry nuclear warheads over Soviet airspace.

The official cover story for the U-2 was that it was a civilian aircraft used to study and gather data on upper atmospheric conditions and weather patterns. Similarly, the first U.S. spy satellite was described as a scientific satellite intended to study the Earth and its environment as part of the International Geophysical Year. When the Eisenhower administration established the National Aeronautics and Space Administration (NASA) in 1958, it invoked the same ruse—a bit disingenuous, considering that not a single astronaut involved in the Mercury, Gemini, or Apollo programs was a civilian scientist; all fifty-five were officers recruited from the United States Armed Forces.

Although Sputnik was an innocuous device, an aluminum sphere about the size of a beach ball that carried a simple radio powered by a battery pack, its impact on America was profound. Getting a satellite into orbit requires a rocket that can reach speeds of approximately 17,000 miles an hour: something scientists call orbital velocity. Since this was beyond the reach of single-stage rockets of that time, Sputnik proved the Soviets possessed a sophisticated multistage rocket capable of reaching the United States.

To quell fears that the US was lagging behind the Soviet Union in science and technology, the Eisenhower administration passed the National Defense Education Act in 1958. The Act provided federal funding to improve instruction in sciences and mathematics at all elementary and secondary schools as well as fellowships for graduate education in the same disciplines. To this day, US students continue to spend a disproportionate amount of time learning advanced math and sciences that most can't apply and will never have reason to use.[95]

---

[95] To the detriment of the Liberal Arts, which impart important lessons on ethics and morality. A similar pattern emerged at the turn of the 19th century: British education stressed the classics while German curricula abandoned the Arts and focused on engineering. We all know how that turned out.

Up to and including WWII, an enemy was someone who lived in an enemy nation or recently emigrated to the US, as was the case of Japanese Americans in 1942.[96] In the 1950s this definition was further expanded to include Americans with communist beliefs. It didn't matter if you acted on them, being suspected was enough to brand you a threat and treat you as such. Many individuals were blacklisted from their professions simply because they had attended or knew someone who had participated in a communist meeting. John Mauchly, the inventor of the ENIAC and EDVAC, was unable to obtain government contracts for the UNIVAC because he had once belonged to the Philadelphia branch of the American Association of Scientific Workers, an organization that, according to the California Committee of Un-American Activities—whoever they were—was formed by the Communist Party as a front to influence legislation restricting the free exchange of information relative to atomic energy. Denied government contracts, Eckert and Mauchly had to sell UNIVAC to Remington Rand in 1950.

Faced with a tangible threat from the Soviet Union and unable to fully ascertain its military preparedness, the Eisenhower administration prioritized R&D spending on surveillance-based technologies and created the Advanced Research Projects Agency (ARPA) to advance these initiatives.

---

[96] Approximately 120,000 Japanese Americans were forcibly incarcerated in ten concentration camps in 1942 following Executive Order 9066, which authorized the relocation and internment of Japanese Americans living on the West Coast.

The Department of Defense Advanced Research Project Agency (ARPA - DARPA)

Of all the agencies established by the US government since its inception, none has impacted America and the rest of the world more than the Advanced Research Projects Agency (ARPA). Created by the US Department of Defense on February 7, 1958, ARPA drew the technology roadmap for the information technology age. Correctly renamed the Defense Advanced Research Projects Agency (DARPA) in 1972, DARPA is unlike any other agency.

Although focused on research and development, DARPA does no direct research. Rather, it monitors academia for new ideas that, if successfully applied, will revolutionize the battlefield. If it can't be used on the battlefield, DARPA won't invest in it. It doesn't matter if a technology has the potential to do a great deal of good; Doing good in not DARPA's mandate.

And that is a problem. When the largest global provider of R&D funds focuses exclusively on battlefield technologies, how much is left for other vital areas of research? Where is the balance and what is the long-term impact on the technology ecosystem? DARPA asserts that many of its technologies are used for peaceful purposes— and that's true. But make no mistake: DARPA technologies are not designed for peaceful purposes. They are created specifically for the battlefield. Warfare is in their DNA, and these technologies are being increasingly woven into the fabric of our private and professional; technologies that don't need to be customized for military and intelligence purposes; all they require is a target.

Global Positioning Satellites (GPS) - *"Aim small, miss small." -* The Patriot (2000)

The story behind GPS is an excellent example of how DARPA fosters the development of cutting-edge battlefield technologies.

When the USSR launched Sputnik in 1957, a small group of doctoral students in the Applied Physics Laboratory (APL) at Johns Hopkins University, who were already engaged in military research funded by ARPA, cobbled together a makeshift receiver to record its transmissions.

The students soon realized that Sputnik's radio signal frequency increased as the satellite approached and decreased as it moved further away. In physics, this shift is known as the Doppler Effect. By studying this phenomenon," the students hypothesized they could accurately track its position from the ground.

The Chairman of the APL, Frank McClure, who had been engaged in military research since 1939, including a stint at the Allegany Ballistics Laboratory where he had been exposed to early computers, was intrigued by their data. He suggested they petition the APL's director for computer time and test their theory. The students also shared their findings with Vanguard—the same Vanguard that the Eisenhower Administration had selected to orbit America's first satellite. Impressed by the student's approach — other US agencies were using radar to track Sputnik's orbit — Vanguard dispatched a representative to consult and obtain more information.

The computer results confirmed the student's theory. The Doppler Effect could be used to accurately determine Sputnik's location from the ground. McClure asked the students if they could invert the process. McClure had spent time in the Navy's Special Projects Office and knew they were having trouble pinpointing the exact location of their Polaris submarines at sea, a piece of information critical to a successful missile strike. McClure reasoned that if a satellite's location could be determined from the ground via the frequency shift of its radio signal, then theoretically the inverse must also be true and the location of a receiver on the ground - or at sea, could be determined by its distance from a satellite. McClure realized this solution could solve the Navy's navigation challenges. Once the students validated his hypothesis, McClure and a colleague wrote a fifty-page proposal and submitted it to the Navy's Bureau of Ordnance.

Initially, the Navy was reluctant to expend funds to test the theory. Their official position was that they did not need improved navigational capability. And so DARPA stepped in to "co-sponsor" the project. It would be responsible for funding the experimental phase, which included the design and construction of the launch vehicles and satellites, sixteen ground stations, and eighteen shipboard receivers, and the Navy would be responsible for operationalizing the system. APL was selected to design the technology, RCA to build it, and Vanguard to launch the finished satellites into space. Six satellites were eventually orbited, three hot units and three spares. Codenamed Transit, it was the forerunner of our current GPS system.

Did you actually think that tens of billions of dollars were spent developing GPS so that you could find the nearest Starbucks? GPS was developed by DARPA and the US Department of Defense to put ordnance on targets.

Corona and Keyhole Reconnaissance Satellites – *"Every move you make, every step you take, I'll be watching you."* – The Police

On May 26, 1955, the US National Security Council reviewed a plan for a series of satellites to replace the U-2 spy plane. President Eisenhower approved the project the following day. The objective was to provide the United States with accurate and timely information about Soviet missile sites, nuclear facilities, and other strategic targets. The first generation of satellites was based on designs by the RAND Corporation. Project subcontractors included Lockheed Corporation, Eastman Kodak, General Electric, Perkin-Elmer Corporation, and Boeing. The USAF and CIA co-managed the program.

Once the satellite's film was exposed, it was ejected and re-entered the Earth's atmosphere in a canister shaped like a bucket. A specially equipped military aircraft retrieved the canister in mid-air as it floated down to the Pacific Ocean suspended by a parachute. The film was rushed to the National Photographic Interpretation Center in Washington, DC, where it was developed and analyzed.

Between 1959 and 1972, 145 CORONA satellites were launched. Approximately two-thirds were successful. The satellite's cameras underwent several revisions during the program's life as new technologies became available. Beginning in 1963 some satellites were equipped with a dual-mode camera. This camera could transmit images to Earth in real-time via a television signal as well as capture images on photographic film for later retrieval.

The KH "Keyhole" series of satellites succeeded the CORONA program. The program's moniker was based on spying into a person's room by peering through their door's keyhole. KH satellites employed electronic imaging sensors, charge-coupled devices (CCDs) that allowed for digital capture and transmission of imagery. CCDs could remain in orbit longer and transmit imagery in near real-time. CCDs were replaced later by Complementary Metal-Oxide Semiconductors (CMOS) sensors. CMOS sensors are more energy efficient and provide excellent image quality, high-resolution, fast autofocus, and better low-light performance. CMOS sensors are used in modern cell phones.

Later satellite designs incorporated advanced microchip technology to reduce payload weight, lower energy consumption, and enhance processing speed. The need for more powerful, energy-efficient, and smaller chips for the space program, satellites, and military aircraft prompted DARPA to fund the research that developed the RISC-based ARM chips used in today's cell phones.

Project Whirlwind

Whirlwind was an MIT project funded by the United States Navy and the Office of Naval Research that began in the 1940s. Its objective was to advance real-time computing capabilities to enhance air defense systems. When the Navy shifted its funding to UNIVAC based projects in the 1950s, the Air Force assumed responsibility for the project. Leveraging advancements achieved by the Navy, the Air Force aimed to develop a real-time operating system capable of integrating data from different systems, such as radar, communications networks, and intelligence databases for air defense.

In contrast to earlier computers that suffered delays due to queuing, Whirlwind's real-time operating system processed data and executed commands immediately upon receipt. Project Whirlwind demonstrated that a modern air defense system could be constructed that was capable of integrating data from disparate air defense systems rapidly enough to permit tracking and interception of incoming threats. Additionally, by incorporating redundant components and fault-tolerant mechanisms, Whirlwind proved enhanced system reliability and ensured operational continuity could be achieved — critical attributes for military systems that require maximum uptime and resilience.

Project Whirlwind laid the foundation for subsequent advancements in real-time computing, operating systems, and interactive computing environments. Sage and Project MAC were built on technologies developed during Whirlwind.

The SAGE Air Defense System

In the early 1950s the USAF began building SAGE (Semi-Automatic Ground Environment): a massive radar-based early warning system to protect North America from high-speed Soviet bombers armed with nuclear weapons. SAGE was the nation's first air defense system and the world's largest computer project.

The SAGE System comprised a network of twenty geographical defense sectors covering the continental United States and Canada. A group of Sectors comprised a NORAD division. Each division was run by one of three Combat Centers which served as senior command headquarters and integrated the individual sectors into the centralized defense system.

Sectors

Each sector was responsible for monitoring and defending a specific region of airspace. The focal point of each sector was the Direction Center (DC). The purpose of the DC was to protect the men and massive computers that monitored the air situation and, if necessary, scramble defense fighters or launch surface-to-air missiles. DCs were huge, four-story, windowless blockhouses constructed of reinforced concrete, partially submerged in the ground and hardened to withstand a nuclear attack. Each of the self-contained DCs—the USAF built 24 of them—housed 3.5 acres of floor space and had its own powerhouse containing large diesel-driven generators, air conditioning equipment, and cooling towers to keep the computer's 50,000 vacuum tubes from overheating.

The entire system was connected by standard telephone lines, many of which were buried underground. Computer data was sent and received from fighter interceptor bases, surface-to-air missile sites, and other facilities via telephone lines equipped with the first Circuit Data Terminal Service (CDTS) modems. At its peak, SAGE was deployed across twenty-seven locations and utilized 25,000 telephone lines.

Total Cost

The cost of developing and deploying SAGE has been estimated at $8 billion; more than three times the cost of the Manhattan Project. This includes the development of radar networks, the construction of DCs and Command Centers, and the design, building, and installation of SAGE's computer systems.

Legacy

Despite the unprecedented effort and national treasure expended on SAGE, the gradual transition from bombers to intercontinental ballistic missiles (ICBMs) seriously degraded its usefulness by the time it was completed in 1963. Nevertheless, SAGE was important for other reasons.

First, SAGE formalized the collaborative framework that America used to create today's massive Defense and Security Establishment. Academia would research, propose, design, and test; private contractors would consult, build, and deploy; and the Department of Defense would fund, direct, and apply. Doubtless, Eisenhower had SAGE in mind when he delivered his farewell address to the nation on January 17, 1961.

Second, SAGE spawned a network of private military contractors who used profits and new technologies generated from defense research to secure additional contracts and to create and dominate global commercial markets for their products and solutions.

For example, between 1952 and 1955, 80% of IBM's computing revenue came from SAGE. It was IBM's largest contract during the 1950s, contributing more than $500 million to its bottom line. But more importantly, IBM used technologies such as the core memory developed for SAGE to become the dominant player in the commercial computer marketplace. Their first non-military system to use magnetic-core memories, the IBM 704, went on the market in 1955.

SAGE was also instrumental in kicking off the software revolution. The software programs written for SAGE were both complex and enormous, even by today's standards. New methodologies, tools, and disciplines had to be developed to create and maintain SAGE's 500,000 lines of code. New companies such as Systems Development Corporation were spun off and thousands of programmers who cut their teeth on SAGE went on to found their own software companies.

Finally, and most importantly, the development of SAGE underscored the urgent need for a new type of communications infrastructure, a more robust "network" that facilitated electronic communications, a requirement that culminated in the creation of the Internet, the foundational technology of our connected world.

The Military-Industrial Complex (1941-1989)

On January 17, 1961, outgoing President Dwight D. Eisenhower appeared on National television to thank the American people for their support, bid them farewell, and offer some counsel based on his fifty years of public service. During his address he coined the term Military-Industrial Complex (MIC), which he defined as "a conjunction of an immense military establishment and a large arms industry."

Since then, there has been much debate regarding the President's comments about the threat posed by the growth of the MIC, almost to the exclusion of his other remarks. This is unfortunate, as it promotes a skewed interpretation of the concerns the President raised, concerns that are still relevant today.

In this chapter, we will revisit Eisenhower's historic address, but this time—thanks to declassified information unavailable to Americans in 1961—within the context of what the President knew about the real Soviet threat and the immense expansion of US Defense and Security Agency capabilities commissioned by his administration to counter it.

For those who didn't live through the 1950s, it's difficult to grasp the full impact the fear of nuclear confrontation had on the world. It left an indelible mark on every aspect of American Society.

"The total influence-economic, political, even spiritual - is felt in every city, every state house, every office of the Federal government."

This fear was exacerbated by the prism through which both sides filtered the confrontation, i.e., as a death struggle between two irreconcilable ideologies rather than what it really was: a struggle between two peoples possessed of different beliefs, beliefs based principally on the suffering they had endured in the period leading up to and including the Second World War.

Eisenhower understood just how deep the fear went. He was aware of Stalin's purges to crush descent in the post-war USSR, and was repulsed by Senator McCarthy and "his" fellow travelers' virulent demagoguery.

"Down the long lane of the history yet to be written, America knows that this world of ours, ever growing smaller, must avoid becoming a community of dreadful fear and hate..."[97]

Immediately upon becoming President in 1953 Eisenhower was assailed by counselors, military and civilian, who sounded alarms about the Soviet threat and the need to take steps, both short-and long-term, to counter it.

"We face a hostile ideology - global in scope, atheistic in character, ruthless in purpose, and insidious in method. Unhappily, the danger it poses promises to be of indefinite duration. To meet it successfully, there is called for, not so much the emotional and transitory sacrifices of crisis, but rather those which enable us to carry forward steadily, surely, and without complaint the burdens of a prolonged and complex struggle, with liberty at stake."

Three months before he became President, the United States successfully carried out Operation Ivy Mike: the

---

[97] A prescient observation, especially when considering the current decline of civility in public debate.

detonation of its first thermonuclear device. Ivy Mike produced a yield of ten megatons, seven hundred times the bomb dropped on Hiroshima. The following year, the Castle Bravo test yielded an incredible fifteen megatons.

"A vital element in keeping the peace is our military establishment. Our arms must be mighty, ready for instant action, so that no potential aggressor may be tempted to risk his own destruction."

During Eisenhower's first term the "bomber gap" posed the greatest threat to National Security. In the second, it was the "missile gap." To meet the former, the US built the SAGE Air Defense System, which, as we have already seen, was a defense initiative of unprecedented proportions. To counter the latter, the US constructed a huge arsenal of short- and long-range nuclear missiles with various yields that could be launched from land or sea.

And yet, as Eisenhower sat before the television cameras that January evening in 1961, he knew that his administration had mistakenly overestimated the Soviet's offensive capability. There had been no bomber gap. In 1956 a U-2 piloted by "Lockheed employee" Marty Newston had flown over a Soviet airbase and photographed thirty long-range Bison bombers. No other Bisons were ever found. Only later did American intelligence experts realize they had been duped. During the Soviet Union's Aviation Day aerial parade in 1956, Soviet pilots had flown the same 20 bombers over the Kremlin in a big circle to inflate the American count. In contrast, the USAF had 160 B-52 long-range bombers in operation by the end of 1956. It was the same with the missile gap. At the time of Ike's address, the Soviet Union had ten to twenty-five launchers. The US had more than one hundred US land-based and sea-based missiles that were forward deployed in allied countries and Polaris submarines.

In its rush to counter the Soviet threat, the US Department of Defense had spent billions—far more than was necessary—to address the real danger. This experience taught Eisenhower a powerful lesson.

"Crises there will continue to be. In meeting them…there is a recurring temptation to feel that some spectacular and costly action could become the miraculous solution to all current difficulties. A huge increase in newer elements of our defense…a dramatic expansion in basic and applied research—these and many other possibilities…may be suggested as the only way to the road we wish to travel. But each proposal must be weighed in the light of a broader consideration: the need to maintain balance in and among national programs…

"In the councils of government, we must guard against the acquisition of unwarranted influence, whether sought or unsought, by the military-industrial complex. The potential for the disastrous rise of misplaced power exists and will persist."

Most people have at least a rudimentary understanding of how the military-industrial complex works—or, more precisely, how it worked in the 1950s.

Until the late 1980s the US military-industrial complex comprised the Department of Defense, its contractors, and the academics that conducted research on its behalf. From the late 1930s until 1958, there was always some quasi-governmental commission that bridged the gap between the three, developing Defense requirements and directing which projects should receive priority. The technocrats who headed these commissions, such as Vannevar Bush and Edwin Land, were extremely influential. Their decisions impacted every almost aspect of America's public and private sectors. They allocated raw materials and set government priorities, determining what would and would not be manufactured. By deciding which technologies to develop, they managed

America's capacity to wage war. When the technologies created for the battlefield were declassified and marketed as commercial products, they also shaped the post-war global economy.

In 1961, Eisenhower, who had begun his career as a West Point cadet fifty years previous, recognized that "[o]ur military organization today bears little relation to that known by any of my predecessors in peacetime, or indeed by the fighting men of World War II or Korea," that there had been a "technological revolution during recent decades" and that while men such as Bush and Land should be held in respect "we must also be alert to the equal and opposite danger that public policy could itself become the captive of a scientific-technological elite."

As the modern battlefield evolved, there was an increasing need for applied technocrats, men who could easily move between the military and its corporate and academic partners, to define defense requirements and help academia and private business meet them.

For example, in an earlier chapter we met Herman Goldstine, a US Army Lieutenant, who in 1943 was working as an ordnance mathematician calculating firing tables at the Ballistic Research Laboratory at Aberdeen Proving Ground in Maryland. Due primarily to his scientific background, Goldstine was appointed liaison between the Army and the researchers who designed ENIAC. After the war Goldstine moved into academia, joining John von Neumann at the Institute for Advanced Study at Princeton. A few years later he was hired by IBM and eventually appointed an IBM Fellow.

Soldiering is a unique profession. To obtain Defense contracts, you need people who understand its requirements and can navigate its command hierarchy. That's why so many senior officers are wooed by the private sector when they retire. As we have already seen, it was Remington Rand that acquired the blacklisted Eckert–Mauchly Computer Corporation (creators of ENIAC, EDVAC, BINAC and UNIVAC) in 1950. To restart its stalled military contracts, Remington Rand appointed General Douglas MacArthur chairman of the board in August 1952. The company had already hired General Leslie Groves, project manager of the Pentagon and Manhattan projects, in 1948.

The uninitiated believe that politicians control Defense spending, which is why private companies hire high-powered lobbyists, but this is patently untrue. Granted, some politicians on various Defense and National Security committees have influence. But not when it comes to actual Defense spending. They can and do influence which base is located where, which ones are closed, and which ones remain active, but as we have already seen and will continue to see as we move through the book, it is the President and his scientific and civilian advisors that determine the extent of the Defense budget—and the Defense Department and its several service arms that decide how to spend it.

This is what the President was really warning Americans against when he said:

"In the councils of government, we must guard against the acquisition of unwarranted influence, whether sought or unsought, by the military-industrial complex. The potential for the disastrous rise of misplaced power exists and will persist. We must never let the weight of this combination endanger our liberties or democratic processes. Only an alert and knowledgeable citizenry can compel the proper meshing of the huge industrial and military machinery of defense with our peaceful methods and goals, so that security and liberty may prosper together."

Despite what an administration believes or hopes to accomplish, it means nothing unless they are willing to provide funding. Money is the power by which governments and individuals exercise choices. The rest is talk. Eisenhower understood that the military-industrial complex posed a threat because of the preponderance of resources and treasure allocated to it.

"We annually spend on military security more than the net income of all United States corporations."

Any budgeter knows that a decision to purchase A is a choice to forgo B. Spending disproportionately on defense promotes a military agenda at the expense of society's more pacific endeavors and endangers our liberty because of the military's imperative for command and control.

This is why Eisenhower made a particular point of lamenting the effect defense spending had on academia. As former president of Columbia University, he knew full well how America's brightest minds were being increasingly drawn into military research and feared the long-term consequences.

"Today, the solitary inventor, tinkering in his shop, has been overshadowed by task forces of scientists in laboratories and testing fields. In the same fashion, the free university, historically the fountainhead of free ideas and scientific discovery, has experienced a revolution in the conduct of research. Partly because of the huge costs involved, a government contract becomes virtually a substitute for intellectual curiosity... The prospect of domination of the nation's scholars by Federal employment, project allocations, and the power of money is ever present and is gravely to be regarded."

Finally, he also understood from his term as the nation's chief executive that America could not keep on spending—and military spending was far and away the largest culprit—the way it was, that; *"[w]e cannot mortgage the material assets of our grandchildren without risking the loss also of their political and spiritual heritage. We want democracy to survive for all generations to come, not to become the insolvent phantom of tomorrow."*

"How can you get a permit to do a damned illegal thing?" - Star Trek III: The Search for Spock (1984)

While the President's remarks provide much insight into the workings of the military-industrial complex, Eisenhower did not address how the US benefited from research obtained from Nazi Germany. Nor did he touch on the process by which state-funded technologies and facilities developed during the war were turned over to private corporations at war's end.

How do you take technologies developed with state funds capable of creating or dominating international markets and make them available to every interested party? Who decide who gets access and who doesn't?

For example: shortly after war erupted on the Korean Peninsula in 1950, the Soviet-built MiG-15 swooped in and began shooting down American B-29s. An exceptional interceptor for its time, the MiG-15 utilized swept-back wings and was powered by a knockoff of the British Rolls-Royce Nene jet engine. The American straight-winged F-80s and F-84s were no match for the MiG, so the US deployed her now-famous F-86 Sabre jet with its own swept-back wing design.

Swept-back wings were a ground-breaking design feature of the Luftwaffe's Me-262, the world's first operational jet fighter, which took to the skies over Europe in 1944. Both the Soviets and Americans seized test data and operational Me-262s from Germany at war's end. If they had intended to crate this materiel and file it away in a massive warehouse in the middle of the desert, as they did with the Ark of the Covenant in *Raiders of the Lost Ark*, they would not have gone to such great lengths to obtain it. So the question remains: how did the US disseminate this information to US aircraft manufacturers? North American Aviation built the F-86, so clearly they were given access. Who else was granted access? And who was denied? Who made those decisions and what criteria were they based on?

Likewise, who decided which companies were given what assets after the war ended in 1945?[98] Certainly, DuPont and GE benefited from the Manhattan Project's research. To this day, GE remains one of the Department of Defense's most important contractors. GE also built a global post-war nuclear reactor business. The passing of privileged information from the state to private industry, the process by which it is accomplished, and the impact it has on determining which companies receive additional Defense contracts and go on to dominate domestic and global markets would be a matter of minor import, of interest only to historians, if it were merely a post-World War II anomaly. But it's not.

In retrospect, Eisenhower's address detailing the threats posed by the military-industrial complex is one of the most remarkable speeches ever delivered by a US President. The dangers he warned us against over sixty years ago are still very much with us today.

---

[98] Does anyone else wonder how the USSR transferred her vast state-owned assets into private hands following the collapse of the Soviet Union?

Project Mathematics and Computation (MAC)

Despite their enormous expense, early computers routinely sat idle for long periods while users entered, checked, or waited on additional data. To reduce downtime, batch processing was invented: a technique in which multiple jobs were consolidated on punch cards or magnetic tape to be processed serially during a single run. Although batch processing reduced downtime, it did not eliminate it; a better solution had to be found.

Based on his exposure to SAGE, MIT professor John McCarthy envisioned a solution where multiple users in different locations could interact with a single computer simultaneously, optimizing expensive computer time. "Timesharing" would require the creation of new software and hardware. The most difficult challenge would be designing an operating system that supported many simultaneous users, where each felt they had exclusive access.

Ultimately, what makes timesharing possible is the speed at which computers operate compared to humans. If it takes a user one second to perform a computation and a computer can do 5,000 computations in the same amount of time, theoretically, 5,000 users could be working on a computer simultaneously. Even though the computer "serves" the needs of each user in turn because it can complete all 5,000 computations in a second, each user feels like they are working in real-time.

Intrigued by the project's potential to increase the efficiency of existing Defense Department computers, tighten security, and reduce costs, ARPA's Information Processing Techniques Office provided funds to the researchers at MIT, and project MAC was born.

Timesharing benefited the Department of Defense by enhancing efficiency, reducing costs, and by consolidating sensitive information from multiple departments on centralized machines. It also revolutionized computer use, moving away from batch processing towards the interactive computing environments with which we are familiar today.

"Lo" it's the ARPANET

In 1962 the Defense Department sponsored a symposium at the Homestead Resort in Hot Springs, Virginia, attended by military research scientists, government contractors, and DARPA officials. By then, most of the challenges of timesharing had been resolved and the researchers were discussing what came next.

Fortunately, the key participants have left accounts of what was said and by whom. In reviewing these conversations, one cannot help but be struck by the clinical way DARPA researchers carried out their work. Like the scientists who built the atomic bomb, or the Nazi rocket scientists who developed the V1 and V2, they seemed to have completely disassociated the nature of their work from the purposes for which it was directed, like doctors who shut down their emotions in order to protect themselves from distress when they inform a patient their illness is terminal.

At Hot Springs, there was a consensus among Pentagon blue jackets and researchers alike that what was needed was a distributed communications network with no single point of failure, resilient enough to survive a nuclear attack. They also needed a network capable of moving large amounts of data, which increasingly included images, at higher speeds and, if possible, more cost-efficiently than the telephone system used by SAGE. Finally, researchers needed a secure way to connect with their peers and, using the timesharing capabilities developed by project MAC, access the specialty applications developed with ARPA funds and hosted at various institutions. For example, UCLA had developed a great simulation capability, Stanford Research Institute specialized in database research, the University of Utah had developed extensive expertise in the use of graphics, and the University of Illinois in high-performance computing.

One of the team's first decisions was to develop a packet-switched network. Ironically, a packet-switching solution had been designed for the USAF in 1962, but because the research was classified, the ARPANet scientists were unaware of it.

Packet switching is a method of sending and receiving data over a network in which the data is divided into smaller, manageable units called packets. These packets contain not only the data being transmitted but also control information, such as the source and destination addresses, sequence numbers, and error detection codes. Packet-switched networks are more robust than switched circuits because they can reroute packets in response to network failures. In contrast, if a dedicated circuit is severed, both the message and the capacity to transmit is lost.[99]

Armed with this solution, the next step was to design a network topology. At first they tried placing low-bandwidth 50kb,[100] leased circuits between the computers in four facilities on the US West Coast, and then connecting each computer to the other three. The problem with this

---

[99] In a spider "web" or "net" severing any strand leaves the rest connected; whereas, cutting a wire breaks it into two unconnected pieces.

[100] As technology progressed, ARPANet's infrastructure was upgraded to support higher data rates. The network saw improvements in speed and capacity, including the use of T1 lines (1.544 Mbps) and eventually higher-speed connections.

topology was that every time a new computer was added to the network, it would have to be connected by a dedicated circuit to all the others. Clearly, this topology would soon prove too unwieldy and expensive. The next solution was to create a looped network where each computer was connected to two adjacent computers in a loop design. Messages would be sent around the loop from computer to computer until they arrived at the target. The challenge with this topology was that if one of the computers went down, the loop was broken, and messaging was disrupted. Finally, they hit on the idea of connecting a small, uniform, military-hardened, mini-processor called an Interface Message Processor (IMP) to each computer to manage its networking functions. Then, instead of connecting the computers with wide-band circuits, they connected the IMPs. This reduced complexity and increased reliability because even if a computer went down, its IMP would continue to relay network traffic.

The first IMP arrived at UCLA on August 30, 1969. The second IMP was delivered to the Stanford Research Institute (SRI) a month later. The units were installed, and a simple test was proposed: an operator at UCLA would attempt to log into the computer at SRI, and a telephone connection would be established between the two facilities so that they could communicate. On October 29, 1969, everything was ready. A scientist at UCLA typed the letter *l*, and the team asked SRI if they could see it. When they replied in the affirmative, the UCLA team typed the letter o. After receiving confirmation that SRI had received it, UCLA typed the letter g, and immediately, the system crashed. Lo – the ARPANet had arrived.

Two more nodes were added later: the University of California, Santa Barbara, the following month and the University of Utah in October 1971.

TCP-IP

By the close of the 1960s nine additional IMPs had been added, linking Defense research facilities on both coasts and bringing the total number of ARPANet nodes to thirteen.

In 1971 a Terminal Interface Processor (TIP) was installed on each coast. TIPs acted as gateways between individual user terminals and the ARPANet, providing all the necessary protocol translation and network access functions to connect directly to the network. This solution permitted users and devices at military facilities to access the network directly rather than through a shared computer environment that might go down.

The original protocol responsible for managing traffic on the ARPANet was called the Department of Defense model. This protocol broke data down into discreet packets and routed them across the ARPANet to their destination address, where the packets were reassembled. A confirmation was then returned to the sending device that the message had been successfully delivered.

As the need arose to connect ARPANET with mobile and satellite networks, a DARPA-sponsored project led to the development a more sophisticated transport protocol, the Network Control Program (NCP). However, the design of NCP was too unwieldy for future needs.

In 1974, researchers introduced a new approach with the specification of TCP (Transmission Control Protocol) and IP (Internet Protocol) as separate protocols. This design aimed to improve the robustness and flexibility of network communication. By 1983, ARPANET officially transitioned from NCP to the TCP/IP protocol suite.

During the early 1980s, other networks such as CSNet, BitNet, and NSFNet began operating, each initially using different communication protocols. However, by the late 1980s, TCP/IP became the standard protocol suite for networking, leading to the formation of what we now recognize as the modern Internet.

In 1984, the Military Network (MILNet)[101] was hived off the ARPANet to provide the Department of Defense with a dedicated network for unclassified communications and, in 1990, what remained of ARPANet was officially decommissioned.

Silicon Valley – *"California Dreamin'"* The Mamas and the Papas

The story of Silicon Valley begins with Fred Terman. Terman earned his undergraduate degree in chemistry and his master's degree in electrical engineering from California's Stanford University before departing for MIT to get his PhD. His advisor at MIT was Vannevar Bush, who, as we have already seen, headed the US Office of Scientific Research and Development during World War II. After graduation in 1925, Terman returned to Stanford. From 1925 to 1941, he designed a course of study in electronics that focused on the building blocks of early computers: vacuum tubes, circuits, and instrumentation.

One of Terman's best students was Bill Hewett, who received his bachelor's degree from Stanford in 1934. There he met David Packard, who earned his B.A. that same year. Hewlett left the following year to attend MIT, where he

---

[101] MILNet was created to separate military network traffic from research network traffic.

graduated with a Master of Science degree in electrical engineering. In 1938, both Packard and Hewlett returned to Stanford, where Packard received his master's degree in electrical engineering, and Hewlett received his post-masters engineering degree.

In 1939, at Terman's urging, Bill and David formed Hewlett-Packard (HP) in a garage in Palo Alto, California. The order of their names was determined by a coin toss. The garage is now a private museum and is considered the birthplace of Silicon Valley.

When the US entered WWII in 1941, Terman moved to Harvard where he headed up the top-secret Radio Research Laboratory established by Vannevar Bush and the OSRD. Terman led a team of eight hundred researchers who developed jammers to block enemy radar, receivers to detect radar signals, and chaff (aluminum strips dropped from planes), to confuse enemy radar.

Hewlett, who had served briefly as Battalion Commander of his high school's Army JROTC program, was also recalled. He served briefly as a signal officer before being transferred to the Army Aviation Ordnance Department. Later, he led the electronics section of the Development Division, part of the War Department's Special Staff.

Under this arrangement, Terman's team did the research, Hewlett managed procurement, and Packard remained at HP, working on Defense contracts. By war's end, HP had 200 employees and was doing $2 million a year in sales. Packard capped his salary at the same level as Hewlett's Army pay. After the war, they returned to Palo Alto, California.

Terman also returned to California and Stanford, where he urged the founding of the Stanford Research

Institute (SRI) in 1946. His goal was to copy Bush's MIT model, obtain Defense grants for research, and encourage graduate students like Hewlett and Packard to found West Coast companies that would turn SRI research into successful high-tech companies. To attract business, Terman convinced Stanford's trustees to establish the Stanford Industrial Park in the Santa Clara Valley on land owned by the University.

Varian Associates, inventors of a vacuum tube that could amplify electromagnetic waves at microwave frequencies, became the first tenant in the Park in 1951. To be close to SRI and the Defense research it was conducting, other major military contractors soon followed, including Hewlett Packard, GE, Eastman Kodak, Lockheed, and Shockley Semiconductor Laboratory.

The Shockley Semiconductor Laboratory was founded in 1955 by William Shockley, an ex-Bell lab researcher who was the co-inventor of the transistor. Funding was provided by Beckman Instruments who later developed analog computers used by the Apollo program. Shockley's main interest was in the four-layer p-n-p-n diode he had conceived at Bell Labs for telephone switching. This direction was at odds with the bright group of young researchers that Shockley had gathered around him; they believed the real opportunity was in producing silicon transistors. Unable to prevail upon Beckman to replace the prickly Shockley, they left the company en masse to found their own company. These men would come to be known as the "traitorous eight."

Now that they were out on their own, the eight's most pressing need was to obtain funding. After several tries with no success, they were eventually introduced to Sherman Fairchild of Fairchild Camera and Instrument who, as we have already seen, was a major defense contractor. Impressed by the smarts and passion of the young men, Fairchild agreed to back them and established the Fairchild Semiconductor division in 1957. In 1959, armed with a grant obtained from ARPA under Project MOSAIC, Fairchild Semiconductor developed the planar process, which involved placing transistors and other components on a single flat surface or plane, laying the foundation for modern integrated circuits. This idea was a breakthrough because it allowed for the scalable fabrication of integrated circuits.

Project MOSAIC played a crucial role in the development of integrated circuit technologies and the growth of Silicon Valley. By the 1960s NASA was sourcing 60% of its integrated circuits from the Santa Clara Valley area. In 1964 alone, they purchased one hundred thousand integrated circuits from Fairchild Semiconductor. A fifth of all military contracts went to companies based in the Santa Clara Valley. By 1965, the Stanford Industrial Park was home to forty companies employing more than eleven thousand four hundred people. By 1992 the United States was responsible for 82% of the world's semiconductor production. As of 2011 nearly five thousand high-tech companies can trace their roots to Frederick Terman and Stanford, including Hewlett-Packard, Cisco Systems, Sun Microsystems, Intel, AMD, Yahoo, and Google.

"Speed is the essence of war." **- Sun Tzu**

Advanced supercomputers are critical for expediting the development and design of new weapon technologies, enabling quicker adaptation to evolving threats and enhancing overall military capabilities on the battlefield.

For example: In 1975 a Skunkworks radar specialist named Denys Overholser unearthed a technical paper authored by Pyotr Ufimtsev, chief scientist at the Moscow Institute of Radio Engineering, entitled *Method of Edge Waves in the Physical Theory of Diffraction*. In it, Ufimtsev took a set of formulas created by a Scottish physicist and refined by a German electromagnetics expert and demonstrated how they could be used to calculate radar cross-sections across the surface of the wing and at its edge to achieve a radar signature so small that it could make an aircraft virtually invisible to radar.

Overholser immediately set to work developing an application to perform these calculations. However, his software could only handle calculations in two dimensions. This limitation arose because, during the 1970s, computing three-dimensional parts would have demanded billions of calculations, exceeding the processing capabilities of computers from that era.

To solve the problem Lockheed created a three-dimensional airplane composed entirely of flat, angular surfaces. Ben Rich, Skunkwork's President, described the Lockheed F-117 Nighthawk's design as a diamond beveled in four directions, creating, in essence, four triangles that resembled an Indian arrowhead when viewed from above.

Today's F-35 has a radar signature comparable to the NightHawk, but in marked contrast to its predecessor, which is comprised of angular panels, the F-35 has rounded surfaces. The difference between these two aircraft is visually startling and is directly attributable to the processing power of the computers used in their design. The development of the Nighthawk also underscores why so many of the first computers were purchased by American aircraft manufacturers.

Cyberspace is ~~tomorrow's~~ today's battlefield...

Red Flag is a graduate course for the USAF's top fighter pilots, conducted at Nellis Air Force Base in Nevada. It employs realistic combat training scenarios to perfect pilot skills and prepare them to become instructors. The course lasts six months, and nearly all of its details are classified.

At the heart of the training facility is a room that houses the Red Flag Mission Debriefing System (RFMDS). The RFMDS uses data captured during training sorties to reconstruct missions in virtual reality so pilots and their instructors can analyze student maneuvers, tactics, and every weapon they drop or fire.

RFMDS originated with 34-year-old Air Force Captain Jack Thorpe. In 1978 Thorpe wrote a paper entitled, *Future Views: Aircraft Training 1980 to 2000,* in which he envisioned a flight training scenario where a squadron of pilots could train for combat using individual, networked flight simulators that allowed all of them to fly in the same battle space.

In this virtual world, pilots would maintain visual and audio contact with one another while a remote commander operated from what Thorpe described as a tactical development center. This center would have a three-dimensional holographic electronic sand table, allowing tacticians and strategists to observe pilots' actions in their simulators.

Bringing Thorpe's vision to life required several years and millions of dollars from DARPA. The new technology revolutionized military training and spawned today's multiplayer gaming market. *RFMDS, Fortnite, Call of Duty,* and *Minecraft* are all based on technology envisioned by Captain Thorpe.

The World Wide Web

Many people use the terms internet and World Wide Web (WWW or W3) interchangeably, but they are two distinct technologies. The internet is a global, distributed digital network of hardware and software that enables data transfer via packet switching. The World Wide Web refers to the vast stores of information accessible via the Internet. Navigating this wealth of data effectively and efficiently demands structured organization and specialized tools such as hypertext, URLs and HTTP.

Hypertext is visually differentiated text, often highlighted with a different color or underlined, that users click on to navigate to the resource referenced by the text. When highlighted text links to another resource through hypertext, it forms a hyperlink. Hyperlinks simplify navigation within or between web pages by concealing the underlying syntax used by computers to redirect users. This syntax, responsible for creating web pages and links, is known as Hypertext Markup Language (HTML).

Uniform Resource Locators (URLs) are unique addresses used to specify the location of resources on the web. They consist of a protocol (e.g., http:// for unencrypted data transfer or https:// for encrypted data transfer where the "s" stands for secure), followed by a domain name (e.g., www.example.com). The domain extension (e.g., .com, .org) signifies the purpose of the domain (e.g., commercial, non-profit).

HTTP stands for Hypertext Transfer Protocol. Protocols are sets of rules governing how systems communicate. For instance, the internet relies on TCP/IP to transmit data packets globally. Similarly, HTTP facilitates the structured organization and retrieval of information accessible via the internet.

HTTP was invented in 1989 by Tim Berners-Lee, a software engineer at the European Organization for Nuclear Research (CERN) in Switzerland. His goal was to create a protocol that simplified the organization and accessibility of documents, making it easier for physicists in remote locations to find and retrieve information stored on centralized computers.

In 1992 the Computer Department at CERN withdrew support for Tim Berners-Lee's WWW project because it did not align with CERN's core mission. To promote the protocol's adoption, CERN released its browser source code under an open-source license on April 30, 1993. Berners-Lee left CERN to join the Massachusetts Institute of Technology (MIT), where he founded the World Wide Web Consortium (W3C) in the fall of 1994. There, he continued to develop the HTTP protocol with funding provided by DARPA.

Early adopters of the World Wide Web were primarily university-based scientific departments and physics laboratories. By January 1993, there were fifty web servers worldwide. Nine months later, there were five hundred.

The Emergence of the ~~Military~~ National Security – ~~Industrial~~ Information Technology Complex (1989 -   )

With the widespread adoption of the internet and the World Wide Web the United States entered the Information Technology Age. What started as a national initiative to create a global defense network capable of deterring Soviet aggression had, by the early 1990s, transformed American industry from manufacturing to an information technology based economy. High Tech companies prospered while America's great industrial cities became ghost towns as manufacturers fled to less developed countries in search of cheaper labor.

The 1990s was not the first time massive defense spending transformed a society. In 1693 French warships savaged a British merchant fleet off the southern tip of Portugal. The disaster sparked a wave of bankruptcies, putting pressure on the King to act. It was obvious to all that England needed to build a modern navy to protect its merchant fleet, but the national treasury was empty. A scheme was hatched to raise capital in which Britons who contributed a minimum of twenty-five pounds would receive an 8% return. Over one million pounds was raised in two weeks, and the Bank of England was born. In 1694, the Bank issued its first loan, and the government ordered a ship-building program of unprecedented proportions.

To meet the demand, new shipyards, and an immense ironworks were constructed. Forges were combined to mass-produce nails and other metal works, and foundries churned out hundreds of cannons. Two thousand trees were used in the construction of every war ship. Vast quantities of iron ore and coal had to be mined and transported to the smelters. Hundreds of miles of rope and canvas sails needed to be manufactured. The surge in factory jobs prompted rural workers to migrate to urban centers in search of higher wages. At the same time, small farms were consolidated to produce the vast quantities of food necessary to victual the expanding Navy.

With a powerful new fleet of warships to safeguard English commerce on the high seas, England became a global economic superpower, importing low-cost raw materials from "underdeveloped" regions in exchange for its higher-value manufactured goods. The treasury overflowed, freeing up additional funds to further expand the fleet. Within seventy-five years, England transitioned from an agricultural to an industrial nation, propelling the world into the industrial era—all thanks to defense spending.

Similarly, in the 1990s, America's economy surged into the information technology age, driven by advanced technologies developed for its defense establishment. In 1995 Netscape's initial public offering raised an astonishing $2.2 billion. Amazon launched its online commerce site in July of the same year, and Microsoft released Windows 95. Windows used a graphical user interface (GUI) to conceal the intricacies of the underlying code from the user, making navigation easier. Windows 95 quickly became a de facto standard, sparking a wave of innovation as developers and entrepreneurs leveraged the operating system to create a wide range of games and desktop applications.

Websites and personal PCs also proliferated. Sun servers powered the internet, while Cisco managed network traffic. IBM became a global blue-chip behemoth, and everyone who was anyone was clicking away on a BlackBerry. Broadband cable debuted, companies automated manual processes and began loading their critical data into Oracle's relational databases. Technological advancements were so rapid that desktop computers became obsolete halfway through their typical three-year lifecycle, and storage media evolved faster than paper records could be converted into digital format.

From an American perspective, this process created a virtuous cycle. The government invested in research and development to produce new technologies for defense. When these technologies were declassified, they were sold by military contractors to private businesses, allied governments, and consumers. This expanded US GDP, reducing the net percentage spent on defense. Selling weapons to allied nations also became a critical business for the Department of Defense because cutting-edge weapons command higher prices, and economies of scale reduce unit costs.

Today, most people believe the Soviet Union collapsed because of its inferior political ideology. But in fact, Glasnost[102] was a product of economic unrest. By 1989, the Politburo could no longer keep pace with Western defense spending without further compromising its domestic living standards.

Andy Warhol was ahead of his time in seeing that America's higher standard of living would trump Soviet ideology. The quintessence of Warhol's genius was not his understanding of how America had used mass production and technological innovation to provide her armies and allies with the means to win the Second World War; it was how these same elements could be used to secure the peace.

In 1962 Warhol founded "The Factory," an art studio where he employed "art workers" to "mass produce" prints and posters of everyday household items such as Campbell's soup, Brillo Pads, and Coca-Cola. Warhol had not only watched the Nixon-Khrushchev kitchen debate, he had grasped its underlying meaning. For Warhol, the proof of America's greatness was not in the pudding—it *was* the pudding.[103]

Warhol understood that the US could spend on Defense without perceptively detracting from America's standard of living, something the Soviet Union was never

---

[102] Glasnost allowed for more public debate and criticism of government policies, which had been suppressed under previous Soviet regimes.

[103] Warhol was ahead of his time. This is what makes his art so valuable today, why collectors are willing to pay millions for a silk screen poster of a Coca-Cola bottle.

able to accomplish. When the Soviet Union collapsed in 1989, about 40% of its GDP was allocated to defense, compared to roughly 5% in the US.

In an insightful scene from Kubrick's *Dr. Strangelove* (1964), the American President questions why the Soviet Union was bent on developing a doomsday device, a weapon so powerful it could destroy the whole world. The Soviet Ambassador responded, "There were those of us who fought against it, but in the end, we could not keep up with the expense involved in the arms race, the space race, and the peace race. At the same time, our people grumbled for more nylons and washing machines."

In-Q-Tel - *"Put some space between us and Bob."* Syriana (2005)

To better understand this next section, envision a man in a basement with earphones and a tape recorder, much like Gene Hackman's character in the 1974 film *The Conversation*, eavesdropping on a telephone call. Instead of focusing on the ethics, consider: is this the most efficient way to tap a phone? Monitoring a single call with an agent is manageable. But what about scaling to hundreds, thousands, or even tens of thousands of calls? What if your ultimate goal is to develop functionality to listen in on every call? After all, how can we be one hundred percent safe unless we monitor every call? Finding answers to these questions is crucial to understanding why we develop specific technologies and it what order.

Returning to the man in the basement: no, it is not efficient. What happens if the conversation is in Russian? We need another agent to translate the call into English. See the dilemma?

Now imagine you are standing in front of a whiteboard in an office at CIA headquarters in Langley, Virginia, considering the manpower problem. The first solution is obvious: instead of dedicating an agent to listen to every call, we record them. And since tapping phones at each location is risky and time-consuming, we order AT&T to give us access to their central telephone exchange. But wouldn't reading a transcript be faster than listening to recordings? What about all those pauses between sentences? Lucky for us, DARPA funded Automatic Speech Recognition (ASR) at MIT during the 1970s. But what if the call is in another language? Again, lucky for us, DARPA funded the Global Autonomous Language Exploitation (GALE) program in the mid-2000s. The GALE program developed technologies for automatically translating and analyzing foreign language documents and speech in multiple languages to support military and intelligence operations. Perfect! Now, we can get a transcript of every call in English, and the whole process is automated. But wait a minute: we still need an agent to read the transcript from every call. How do we solve that one? DARPA has the answer for that one, too. It's called Artificial Intelligence. DARPA has been funding Artificial Intelligence (AI) research since the 1950s. And they have gotten so good at it that we can take all those transcripts and wash them through AI algorithms that look for red flags in computer nanoseconds. Not only that, these applications are self-learning, so the more data we analyze, the better we can tune them to identify patterns that interest us. Even better, we can claim that we are not technically violating US privacy laws because no human looked at the transcripts!

So where did Google get its speech-to-text, translation, and AI technologies? Say hello to In-Q-Tel. In-Q-

Tel is a strategic investment firm that functions as the venture capital arm of the United States Central Intelligence Agency (CIA). In-Q-Tel was established in 1999 with the primary mission of identifying and investing in cutting-edge technologies to enhance the capabilities of the CIA and other US intelligence agencies.

So again, imagine you are the CIA or the NSA, and you are collecting more data through your surveillance activities than you can effectively analyze. You need a search engine to quickly plow through all the data and organize results according to relevance. Luckily for the US Security Establishment, two PhD students studying large-scale distributed systems and data mining at Fred Terman's Alma Mater, Stanford University, developed a PageRank algorithm in a research environment funded by DARPA's Digital Library Initiative.

When you put all these pieces together, you understand why specific technologies were developed and in what order. In the early days of computers, the Defense Department tasked researchers to find solutions. But by the 1990s, there were enough technology companies and research students studying computer science, that it became more efficient to get them to build the technology, start companies, and then purchase "their" technology.

And that is how In-Q-Tel works. In-Q-Tel looks for start-ups or researchers developing technologies that could prove valuable to the US Security Establishment and provides them with funding and access to other "resources." In return, they hold stock in these companies. Some succeed, and some don't. But because the CIA gets in on the ground floor, the ones that take off more than pay for the failures. How In-Q-Tel manages the bookkeeping no one but In-Q-Tel can say. Certainly the CIA has not always been transparent about its accounting practices in the past. We have already seen how they used hidden slush funds and third party contractors to pay for their   U-2 project and spy satellite programs.

And what of those other resources? Imagine you are working at the CIA, where you dream of extending your intelligence-gathering capabilities to cell phone users in every country. Social media provides the perfect solution. In-Q-Tel approaches Twitter and tells them they have a small group of data scientists who are developing AI algorithms specifically for analyzing social media to identify breaking news, validate it, and provide near real-time alerts to interested parties. The CIA makes the introductions and brings the two parties together. The data scientists are given a backend connection to Twitter's servers to get tweets in real-time and tune their AI algorithms. This is how Dataminr was created. Today, Dataminr monitors hundreds of thousands of social media sites in almost every country. So if the Soviets move troops in Ukraine and a Ukrainian tweets or posts a picture of that movement to almost any social media site, Dataminr picks up the post and passes it along. This is an excellent example of how In-Q-Tel fosters new technologies and then leverages them for intelligence gathering purposes.

But this is not our the chief concern; the real issue for the American people is what information the Department of Defense and the Security Establishment share with America's largest corporations. For example: how much of Google's map capability was provided by the Department of Defense? Likewise, did they develop their speech-to-text capability or translation software from scratch or was it, or some part of it, provided by Defense or another US security agency?

Ten years ago you could go to the cottage for the weekend and there was no cell phone coverage. Soon, that will be a thing of the past. Starlink will ensure that you will have coverage no matter where you are on the planet. But is that the primary reason it is being built? Yes and no. Part of Starlink is Starshield, the military division, designed for government use. The military needs coverage wherever its forces are deployed. They also need a distributed satellite network with no single point of failure, like the internet, capable of moving vast amounts of data that will continue functioning when individual nodes are destroyed. So they provide StarLink with technologies to put its satellites into orbit.

Bringing us back to the conundrum of how does the government decide which companies to assist? How do you compete in a free market where a small group of defense contractors has privileged access to billions of dollars of classified R&D? How far does that information sharing go? What are the connections between the defense agencies and America's largest corporations?

During World War II, the US Army Air Forces launched a strategic bombing campaign called Daylight Precision Bombing to destroy the German Luftwaffe and the industrial base that sustained it. They started by bombing aircraft assembly plants, then moved on to the factories that manufactured critical components, such as the propeller works at Anchan. In 1943 they raided the ball bearings works at Schweinfurt and Regensburg—ball bearings, the planners reasoned, were essential to German war production. Later they extended the campaign to oil refineries and synthetic plants. In the lead-up to the D-Day invasion, they bombed bridges and railyards in occupied France. On May 27th, 1942, the Mighty 8th bombed Cologne, causing consternation in the ranks of the aircrews as strategic bombing, in contrast to Bomber Command's "city busting," was supposed to bomb strategic targets and avoid civilian casualties. And yet, by the end of the war, the 8th Airforce combined with Bomber Command to destroy Dresden which, by February 1945, was predominantly a non-military target choked with refugees. Clearly the definition of what constituted a strategic target changed as the war continued. If it's ok to bomb a factory or a railyard, then why not the homes of the men who work there?

The bombing of Germany during WWII demonstrated the link between the military and the industries that sustain it. If a ball bearing plant was critical to Germany's national security in 1943, then how essential is Amazon or Google to America's national security today?

"Corruption? We have laws against it precisely so we can get away with it. Corruption is our protection. Corruption keeps us safe and warm...Corruption is why we win." - **Syriana (2006)**

In 2013 Canada's intelligence agency was caught hacking the computers at Brazil's Ministry of Mining and Energy. At the time Brazil was seeking to auction off the rights to help Petroleo Brasileiro, Brazil's state oil company, develop its newly discovered Libra Oil Field, a find estimated to contain eight to ten billion barrels of oil.

When the bidding closed, none of the major oil companies from the Five Eyes countries, a shared intelligence community of the US, UK, Canada, Australia, and New Zealand, had placed bids. What did the Canadian government learn from those computers? How did that information end up in the hands of private oil company executives? And what was Canada doing spying on Brazil's Ministry of Mining and Energy in the first place?

Oil is a vital natural resource, and Canada is a leading producer. In fact, oil is so essential to the global economy that the US Department of Defense has more personnel and equipment stationed in the Middle East than in any other region.

National economies are the engines that provide revenue to the state. If the economy is strong, there is money to spend on everything else, including defense. If it is weak, every government department is negatively impacted. How far should governments go to succor the private companies that constitute the backbone of their economy?[104] Should they be using state revenue and resources to spy on foreign corporations on behalf of domestic corporations? Where do you draw the line between your own economic security and international fair play? Or are there no more lines anymore?

Total Information Awareness – *"One last screw."* - The World is Not Enough (1999)

Just as American drone strikes on Arab nationals can't be equated to terrorist attacks, the Arab attacks on the US in 1993 and 2001 can't be labeled "terrorist" acts aimed at symbolic targets. Recognizing this distinction is crucial because how we perceive threats determines our response to them.

All twenty-five men involved in both attacks were Sunni Muslims. Fifteen of the nineteen participants in the 9/11 attacks were Saudis. Of the remaining four who were not Saudis, three were pilots of the hijacked planes. All four received flight training at private schools in the US in the

---

[104] A question Canadians asked but never received answers to in an investigation into the SNC-Lavalin scandal.

months leading up to the attacks, suggesting that the attacks were driven by a shared belief that the US opposes "true" Islam, that the attacks were meticulously planned well in advance and that the Saudi nationals recruited outsiders only because they needed individuals with particular skills or the ability to acquire them.

These men were not attempting to induce terror by targeting civilians. They were well-prepared and well-funded, and their attacks specifically targeted America's political, military and economic power triumvirate – viz the U.S. Capital buildings, the Pentagon and the World Trade Center.

More Americans were killed in the 9/11 attacks than by the Japanese at Pearl Harbor. It was more than just a "terrorist" attack; it was a strike at the very heart of the nation.

To protect Americans against future threats the Bush Administration created the Office of Total Information Awareness (TIAO) in 2002. The mission of the TIAO was to oversee the Total Information Awareness (TIA) program, an initiative proposed by DARPA and headed by Admiral John Poindexter. The objective of the TIA was to develop and integrate advanced technologies for comprehensive data collection and analysis to enhance national security by detecting and preventing potential threats.

The scope of the information assets the agency wanted to access was unprecedented, including emails, text messages, internet browsing histories, images, videos, social media postings, metadata related to electronic communications—where individuals were located, with whom and when—banking transactions, credit card usage, bank statements, airline reservations, travel itineraries, transportation records, tolls paid, travel patterns, biographical data, employment history, educational background, information from surveillance cameras and satellites, information contained in public records, databases such as passports and driver licenses, any registered businesses, or any other organizations they may be members of, properties, housing, medical records, prescriptions, retina scans, gait analysis, images that can be used for facial analysis, magazine subscriptions, and more.

Because most of the details about TIA remain classified, there is no way of accurately ascertaining the number of individuals the agency targeted or how many were US citizens. Nor do we know the extent to which they planned to anonymize the data (scrub it for tombstone data such as name, birth date, etc.) or how long the data would be retained.

What we do know is that there was a significant public backlash against this unprecedented invasion of American privacy rights. In response, the Bush administration disingenuously rebranded the TIA as the Terrorism Information Awareness Office, attempting to underscore the need for extreme measures by presenting them as indispensable to combat "terrorism." Despite these efforts to mollify its critics, Congress defunded the Information Awareness Office in late 2003.

We also know from information released by former NSA employee and whistle blower Edward Snowden that after the demise of the Office of Total Information Awareness, the NSA either incorporated the bulk of the technologies developed for TIA into its own systems or re-created them, and that they are currently engaged in collecting vast amounts of data on American citizens under a program called PRISM.

Google Earth

Keyhole, Inc. was founded in Mountain View, California in 2001. The company specialized in geospatial data visualization software. Their application, EarthViewer, rebranded later as Keyhole 2 LT, was a SaaS based 3D computer model that let users zoom in and virtually explore the earth. In 2003, In-Q-Tel, in partnership with the National Geospatial Intelligence Agency (NGA), the government agency responsible for providing geospatial intelligence to support national security objectives, invested in Keyhole. Using the existing product as the base engine, Keyhole, and the NGA co-developed functionality to import additional data into the program: weather, military installations, troop movements, etc., providing war-fighters and intelligence analysts with a near-real-time, mashup of the battlefield that can be seamlessly shared across agencies. In 2004, Google acquired Keyhole 2LT and rebranded it as Google Earth.

Google Earth's creation illustrates how the relationship between US intelligence agencies and high-tech companies is evolving. Rather than providing money to researchers and scientists to develop new technologies, the CIA becomes a stakeholder and brings together the parties necessary to build out solutions. Together they operationalize them and sell them back to private industry. This allows the CIA to profit from the sale, put some distance between themselves and the private companies who do the work for them, use the solution without paying to maintain it, take advantage of upgrades as the company continues improving the product, and benefit from economies of scale as companies like Google acquire additional customers. It is also a win for Google because it gives them a footprint in the defense and security community, a lucrative vertical they have been steadily expanding since 2004.

Social Media – "lovit' volka na tsyplonka." John Wick (2014)

When I was growing up in the late 1970s, my future father-in-law would come home from work, lie on the couch, and read the local newspaper while waiting for dinner. The last thing he did each night before bed was watch the national news on network television. These were the primary media sources that shaped his worldview. Both were regulated. The conduct of journalists was enforced by editorial policy based on ethical standards set by journalistic organizations and associations. TV and advertising were regulated by government-appointed commissions, such as the Federal Communications Commission (FCC). Governments established these regulatory bodies because they understood how powerful media was in shaping public opinion.

The Nazis used the media to indoctrinate the German people and demonize their enemies. The Communists use it for ideological control and state censorship. In a democracy, a free press is supposed to hold governments and powerful institutions accountable, provide diverse viewpoints, and facilitate informed public debate.

Because the media can be such a powerful tool for shaping public opinion, intelligence agencies have regularly used it to destabilize unfriendly regimes.

For instance: Jacobo Árbenz was elected President of Guatemala in March 1951. His administration's flagship policy was an agrarian reform bill designed to expropriate sections of large landholdings, mainly owned by America's United Fruit Company. United Fruit was to be compensated based on past property assessments used for tax purposes and the land redistributed to impoverished agricultural laborers.

The Eisenhower administration, alarmed by the number of Communist advisors in the Árbenz government, and a reform bill they construed as the thin edge of a Communist wedge, signed off on a covert campaign proposed by the CIA to overthrow him.

"The plan of operations called for cutting off military aid to Guatemala, increasing aid to its neighbors, exerting diplomatic and economic pressure against Arbenz and attempts to subvert and or defect Army and political leaders, broad scale psychological warfare and paramilitary actions."[105]

The CIA chose Carlos Castillo Armas, an exiled, ex-Guatemalan Army officer, to lead the coup. They also air-dropped pamphlets calling for Árbenz's resignation and saturated the airwaves with fake reports of a rebel army converging on the capital. The generals, convinced that Árbenz could not hold out against a rebel force backed by the United States, urged him to resign, which he did on 27 June 1954.

The CIA used similar tactics to remove Iranian Prime Minister Mohammad Mossadegh in 1953 and defeat the Italian Communist Party in the 1948 Italian general elections.

During the same period, the Soviets routinely planted fake news stories in newspapers and magazines at home and abroad to undermine confidence in the US Government. The Soviets called these campaigns "Active Measures."

---

[105] "Operation PBSUCCESS" The United States and Guatemala 1952-1954.

From Mass to Social Media

In contrast to the local and national outlets that informed Americans before the proliferation of the internet, today's social media is international in scope. The app you interact with is the same platform used worldwide. People use social media to share updates, stay connected, follow news, and enjoy entertainment. Advertisers and interest groups leverage it to sell products and sway opinions, while social media executives profit by convincing these advertisers and groups that they know their users better than the competition.

They achieve this by modeling user behavior. Social media platforms record, track, measure, and analyze everything you do: your friends, acquaintances, locations, vacations, every ad you've clicked on, every survey you've filled out, your likes, dislikes, every picture or video you've viewed, and how long you viewed it. It also takes note of the friends who appear in your photographs and how frequently, the relationship you have with each friend, your chats, your comments, and much more. This information is used to infer what kind of person you are, such as whether you are sociable or introverted, your political affiliations, religious beliefs, and even your emotional state. The more data you provide, the more accurately you can be profiled. The ultimate goal is not to predict what you will do, but to identify the most effective way to get you to take a specific action. DARPA puts it this way; "DARPA's mission is not to predict the future, but to create it through breakthrough technologies."

That's why DARPA funds the Persuasive Technology Lab at Stanford University, a "requisite" course for social media executives and developers. The lab's research focuses on understanding how technology can be designed to influence human behavior persuasively through mobile apps, websites, and other digital interfaces. The Persuasive Technology Lab leverages persuasive design principles for both commercial and defense-related purposes.

This is where the US Intelligence Community's interests lie. Based on the PRISM slides leaked by Edward Snowden, the CIA has had access to Facebook's user data since 2014. As we have already seen, the CIA effectively used 1950s media to destabilize governments and influence foreign elections. The targeted modeling data collected from today's social media platforms makes their capabilities even more formidable because they can now tailor their operations to individual users.

This also helps explain America's growing polarization. Like the CIA, foreign agencies also exploit social media to spread fake news, sow discord, and undermine trust in our government. Their work is made easier by the fact that users are more likely to click on outrageous stories than on everyday news. The success of these "Active Measures" can be gauged by the growing number of Americans who believe the world is flat, that the moon landings were faked, or that the US Government conspired with the 9/11 attackers. The confusion is further compounded by personalized feeds that give every user a different perception of reality.

During WWII America waged three-dimensional warfare: war on land, sea, and air. When the Pentagon began weaponizing space in the 1950s, warfare became four-dimensional: land, sea, air, and space. Today, the US Intelligence Community refers to warfare in five dimensions: land, sea, air, space, and information.

Artificial Intelligence (AI) - David: *"Is this a game or is it real?"* WOPR: *"What's the difference?"* - WarGames (1983)

Artificial Intelligence, the simulation of human intelligence in machines programmed to think and learn like humans, has been the dream of scientists and researchers since the advent of the computer. In 1950, Alan Turing, a British mathematician and computer scientist who helped crack the German Enigma code during WWII, introduced the Turing Test to evaluate a machine's ability to exhibit human-like intelligence through text-based interactions, where subjects tried to distinguish between machine and human responses. Similarly, in 1948, John von Neumann envisioned a "universal constructor"—a self-replicating machine capable of emulating human cognitive abilities. These visionary concepts laid essential groundwork for the development of artificial intelligence.

Since its inception, DARPA has provided ongoing funding to develop AI technologies based on their potential to enhance battlefield capabilities and national defense. During the 1960s it funded projects such as the Logic Theorist by Allen Newell and Herbert A. Simon, which was among the first programs to use heuristics and symbolic reasoning, and Shakey the Robot, an early mobile robot equipped with vision and planning capabilities. In the 1980s DARPA launched the Strategic Computing Initiative to develop high-performance computing and AI systems, which included projects such as the Autonomous Land Vehicle, a precursor to self-driving cars. In 2012 DARPA funded the Deep Learning program to develop deep neural networks capable of learning from large datasets, leading to breakthroughs in speech recognition and image classification.

Perhaps the best way to understand AI is to refer to the section where we explored timesharing. Timesharing leverages the speed of computers to interact with multiple users concurrently, giving each user the perception of real-time interaction. AI leverages computer clock speeds to accelerate learning.

For example: imagine playing chess against a machine that can calculate every move available to both players before each turn. Now picture that same computer simultaneously playing 100 games with different players and learning from each game. At that rate, it won't take long for the computer to outperform even the best player. Now, take that same learning model, and instead of playing chess, use it to teach a modern jet fighter how to dogfight. The only limit on how fast and how well it will learn is the volume and quality of input data.

But this is just the beginning. The chess and fighter plane examples are more machine learning than artificial intelligence. True artificial intelligence focuses more on accomplishing missions than performing tasks. An autonomous drone can make decisions independently with minimal human intervention, navigate obstacles, and adjust to unforeseen circumstances.

Autonomous devices can also learn to function in groups or "swarms," like a swarm of bees defending their nest from an intruder; some bees will be killed but the others will continue to sting. Apply the same logic to a squadron of unmanned attack helicopters programmed to destroy an enemy surface-to-air missile battery, and it's easy to see why DARPA has such a keen interest in AI.

The UN is currently debating the ethical and humanitarian implications of allowing machines to make autonomous decisions to kill without meaningful human control. Critics are concerned that autonomous systems lack the nuanced judgment and ethical considerations inherent in human decision-making, posing a higher risk of civilian casualties and unintended escalation of conflicts. Proponents argue that lethal autonomous devices have already been used in conflicts in Ukraine and Syria. They want to shift the debate to defining clear boundaries and regulations for their use.

At the Pentagon, the Defense Department is focused on integrating AI into its military decision-making architecture through initiatives like the Army's Project Convergence, the Navy's Overmatched, and the Air Force's Advanced Battle Management system. The goal is to leverage battlefield data preprocessing to accelerate and improve decision-making for commanding officers. This aligns with Colonel John Boyd's decision-making model, known as the OODA loop, which aims to achieve a competitive advantage in warfighting through a rapid cycle of observing, orienting, deciding, and acting. By disrupting an opponent's decision-making processes, it keeps them reactive and at a disadvantage. The stunning success of the ground offensive in Operation Desert Storm was largely attributed to the practical application of Boyd's OODA loop strategy.

The predecessors of these technologies are used by applications on your phone to analyze information about you. It used to take days for those running shoes your son was looking at on his phone to show up in your feed. Now, it happens in minutes. Your phone knows who he is, who you are, who you are to him, and that you are the one who will decide if he gets the shoes. It can even score how likely you are to purchase. Look on the bright side: at least it is not a killer drone.

Digital IDs – *"One ring to rule them all."* - J.R.R. Tolkien, The Fellowship of the Ring

One of the primary objectives for writing this book is to help the reader understand the logic that led to the development of current technologies. Understanding what came before and why helps us predict what comes next. For example; for several years an international movement has been underway to develop a universal digital ID. If you believe its advocates, the absence of a unique identifier is holding the world back, costing governments billions to maintain duplicate databases and, therefore, keeping governments and humanity from reaching their ultimate potentials. Digital IDs, they argue, will make it possible for global leaders to build the ultimate system where every piece of information about every person is linked to their digital IDs. Can't get a bank account because you don't have ID? No problem; you can use your digital ID. Are you a refugee seeking assistance? All you have to do is present your digital ID. Want to travel to another country? Your digital ID links to your vaccine records. Need government assistance? Just show them your digital ID.

Consider all the systems you access daily. Almost all require a unique username and password. To reduce complexity, most large organizations use Single Sign-On software, where users create a single username and password, which is stored in a central database for retrieval as needed. This gives the company one set of credentials to manage, making it easier for users to traverse the various systems they need to do their jobs. Should the need arise, user access can be severed with the click of a mouse.

That may not matter much in the workplace, but what happens if we apply the same logic to your internet access? Every node on the internet has a unique identifier issued by the Internet Assigned Numbers Authority (IANA). No two devices can use the same identifier simultaneously. Think of it like a telephone number: the identifier constitutes a chokepoint because without it you wouldn't be able to get online.

Now imagine you are your own unique identifier. There would be no need for usernames, passwords, pay services, debit or credit cards, and no possibility of identity theft or fraud. You will be able to go anywhere and do anything. All that needs to be certified is you. Of course, this technology will necessitate the introduction of standardized interrogators at the store, at the workplace, in the rental car, and probably at your own front door. And there will be no way to opt-out or argue because scanners aren't human; no ID, no access.

Ironically, this is actually one of the arguments used to *promote* digital IDs. If you use a card to make a purchase, how does the system confirm that the card belongs to you? Digital IDs will solve that problem. That is why they argue that your digital ID has to be linked to a biological, because without that connection it becomes just another ID subject to identity theft and fraud.

The first global initiative to develop a "universal ID" had three main sponsors: a high-tech giant, an international philanthropic organization, and a pharmaceutical company. The need for the first two is obvious; someone has to develop the tech and someone has to pay to develop the technology. But why a pharmaceutical company unless they envision a biological component?

In the Book of Revelation, Chapter 13:16-17 it reads:

"And he causeth all, both small and great, rich and poor, free and bond, to receive a mark in their right hand, or in their

foreheads: And that no man might buy or sell, save he that had the mark..."

I have always been impressed by this passage, not so much because of what it says but who said it. The writer lived on a tiny island 2,000 years ago where transactions were based on the odd silver coin or barter. And yet he said he saw that everybody had to receive a mark to buy or sell and that the mark was somehow part of their bodies.

Digital IDs represent a watershed technology. Once issued, they can't be revoked. The technology required to implement them is readily available, and based on the development trajectory of new technologies it is highly likely that they will be introduced. While this may seem speculative, there is precedent. During the COVID-19 pandemic, there was tremendous governmental and social pressure on people to get vaccinated. Legally, you didn't have to comply, but you couldn't travel, attend social events, or dine out without showing proof of vaccination. The same pressures will probably be used to get people to accept digital IDs.

Central Bank Digital Currencies (CBDC) – *"You'll own nothing, and you'll be happy."*

Regardless of the propaganda currently being circulated by Central Banks, digital currencies represent the greatest threat to individual freedom ever contemplated. In contrast to currency, CBDCs cannot be possessed; they can only be used—a critical distinction. Because currency can be possessed, it can be exchanged on a peer-to-peer basis. Both parties in the transaction are autonomous. They can buy and sell without consent from any outside party. This is not the case with CBDCs. You cannot own a digital currency, you can only use them. And because you can never own them, they can never be used without the consent of the issuing authority. Despite all the claims of central bankers that CBDCs are just like debit cards or cash—that they are easier to use, more efficient, faster, more secure, and that they are going to do away with terrorism and money laundering—CDBCs are not the same. Because, unlike cash or debit cards, every purchase you make requires government assent.

Ironically, the retort to this criticism is, "If a transaction is denied, you can always use another form of currency." "Digital currencies," they say, "will not replace fiat currency." Then why are they developing them? What are they going to replace?

Given that you will lose the ability to do any transaction without government permission, do you really want to take that chance? Do you really believe any government will support two different forms of currency?

During COVID, truckers in Canada launched a protest movement called the Freedom Convoy. To quell the unrest, the government invoked emergency powers—Canada's War Measures Act—and froze the bank accounts of hundreds of protestors.

If you have ever been part of a protest or watched how politicians respond to them, you know how loathe they are to use force to quash them. This is because, in the West at least, governments are democracies; their right to govern is derived from the people. When the police or the military start clubbing demonstrators, the politicians can see the sand running out of the hourglass of their administrations. That's why freezing bank accounts is so powerful—so powerful in fact that Canada's Prime Minister had to invoke the War Measures Act to do it. Protestors could no longer buy gasoline, purchase food, or take care of their dependents. It is the worst kind of coercion because it isolates its victims, permitting the state to enforce its will without fear of public backlash.

CBDCs will give the government that power and more. As long as there is currency, dissenters can resist, and supporters can donate money to support protest groups and those who head them. Not so with CBDCs. They will be tied to a unique identifier, probably a biological one. They cannot be used to support anything or anyone that the government disapproves of.

Exercising this kind of control is easy because CBDCs are programmable. What you can do with them will depend on your user settings; just like China today. You can buy a ticket to go here, but if you try to buy a ticket to there, the purchase will be "frustrated."[106] You can buy that but not this. You can buy this much of that but no more. That is the power of CBDCs. They are nothing like cash or debit cards.

In the digital era, CDBCs represent the end game. CDBCs will give governments the power to extend beyond surveillance to control. CDBCs are the last domino of a "user-based" society.

Bitcoin – *"I can go now."* Heart and Souls (1993)

The emergence of Bitcoin may well be one of history's most fascinating cloak-and-dagger stories. Shortly after the 2008 financial meltdown, Satoshi Nakamoto—a pseudonym for an anonymous person or group of persons—published a seminal blueprint for a blockchain database. And just to ensure that everyone got the message, they embedded the following in Bitcoin's first block: "The Times 03/Jan/2009 Chancellor on brink of second bailout for banks."

---

106 The euphemism the World Bank has adopted to describe the process of declining a payment.

Don't be confused by all the hype around cryptocurrency. It's not about Bitcoin; it's about the blockchain it runs on. In contrast to fiat currencies, Bitcoin's ledger operates on a distributed network. It resides on hundreds of thousands of computers, with no central bank ownership and no single computer that can be hacked. Consequently, Bitcoin can be accessed from anywhere, and no government can control it.

That's why a single Bitcoin is worth tens of thousands of dollars: it's a hedge against Central Bank Digital Currencies (CBDCs). As long as there is Bitcoin, individuals can buy and sell without government permission in any country. To grasp Bitcoin's significance all you have to do is observe how China's Communist Party is using the digital Yuan to tighten its grip on its people.

So, who are the authors of Bitcoin? Several things stand out when reviewing Satoshi's emails: first, it takes very sophisticated technology and the knowledge to use it to remain anonymous, especially when some of the world's best hackers are trying to find you. Second, the authors prioritized establishing a community of developers to drive Bitcoin's development, as if they were intentionally laying the groundwork for the project. Why didn't they do it themselves? Why did they need a third party? Third, the way the author communicated with third-party developers was indicative of interrogation training. Coincidence can and does happen, but tradecraft is unmistakable.

This begs the question: why would an intelligence agency want to create Bitcoin?

When the markets crashed in 2008 governments worldwide injected billions of dollars to keep their currencies from collapsing. Those billions went to making interest payments, not paying debt. In fact, debt mushroomed after 2008. Think of it like a credit card. As long as you keep making your payments, the bank raises your limit. But miss a payment, and they are on the phone. Wealthy investors don't care about their capital; they care about the *return* on their capital. Interest payments keep the economy rolling.

Post World War I Germany is a perfect example of how this cycle works. When the war ended in 1918, the Allied nations demanded compensation for injuries inflicted on them by the Germans. When the Germans could not pay, America, the principal creditor, twice provided loans to the Germans so they could make their minimum payments. It didn't matter that the Germans made interest payments with borrowed money as long as they kept making them.

This is why American bankers used the colloquialism of "kicking the can down the road" to describe their handling of the 2008 financial crisis. They did stave off disaster, but they had to incur even more debt to do it. Next time, it will be much worse.

The US dollar is the world's de facto global reserve currency, used widely for international trade and held by central banks as a primary reserve asset. If it collapses, as it almost did in 2008, it would bring down the global economy and there would be no practicable way to save fiat currencies. That's why central banks are developing digital currencies. They realize that unless debt is brought under control, sooner or later, it will become impossible to refinance it. This will cause a run on banks the like of which the world has never seen. The social unrest that would result is imponderable.

How a worldwide economic collapse would impact people's freedom in different countries will ultimately depend on the extent of the unrest and how their governments respond. But one thing is sure: in that brave new world, the only things standing between freedom and totalitarianism will be barter and Bitcoin.

Maybe it will never happen. Maybe the intelligentsia is correct; perhaps debt and inflation are just theoretical abstracts and we can keep printing money forever. But be that as it may, all the evidence to date suggests that the emergence of Bitcoin was an intelligence-sponsored operation timed to coincide with the release of the digital Yuan and precede the introduction of CBDCs in other countries.

How the Military Created Your Phone - and Why That Matters

Remember when you got your cell phone? You took it out of the box, powered it on, and were presented with a user agreement. If you are like most people, you never read it. You just nodded your head and clicked accept. Think about that for a moment. What did you accept? The terms and conditions of its use, or the fact that you are a user? Not an owner, a user. Think about how different that is from everything else you purchase. When you buy a house, car, or snow shovel, you are an owner. But when you buy a phone, you are a user. The same thing happens when you buy a new TV. You can't stop ads from appearing on it – because you are not an owner anymore, you are just a user. In fact, every time you connect to the internet, you are a user.

The Department of Defense created the internet to command and control its assets. Computers, radar stations, ballistic missile silos, air bases, satellites, troops in the field— all of these are assets. When you connect to the internet you, too, become an asset. You don't notice it because it happens in the background. You make calls, send messages, and check your feeds. But everything you do on your phone is tracked, measured, and recorded.

Most of this tracking is accomplished through third parties such as your carrier, Facebook, Instagram, YouTube, Gmail, Google, Waze, Amazon, and Spotify. These companies constantly collect information about you, model that data, and sell it to others. Their value proposition is knowing more about you than their competitors. This is the value they sell to advertisers. This is how they make money. They work for hire.

Not so with the Defense Department. They paid to develop the ARPANet and the technologies that power your phone. In-Q-Tel invests in ventures that create the technologies third parties use to encrypt, collect, model, measure, and track user data. The question is: why? Why has the US government spent trillions of dollars developing these technologies? What do they get in return? The ability to detect, track, and counter threats. But what constitutes a threat is a matter of perspective.

In a democracy, you are innocent until proven guilty. In the military, everyone is a threat until proven otherwise. In the military, power flows from the top down; in a democracy, it flows from the bottom up. In the military, secrecy is imperative; in a democracy, it is dangerous. The military protects us from threats from without; democracy protects us from threats from within.

Since the Soviet Union detonated her first atomic device in 1949, the United States has been living under the shadow of the mushroom cloud. To counter that threat, she built a security apparatus so ubiquitous that it has literally transformed every aspect of our society and propelled the world into the Information Technology age. Today, America spends more on defense than the next nine largest countries combined.

This imbalance is subtly corrupting the way Americans see themselves and the rest of the world. We are starting to look more like a military state than a nation based on individual rights and freedoms.

We have expanded our definition of what constitutes a threat to everyone, spying on our allies and hacking the cell phones of their political leaders. We steal industrial secrets and share them with our corporations, ensuring American companies prevail in global markets. We clandestinely gather bulk data on every American - including minors, analyze that data using sophisticated AI algorithms, and then skirt the Fourth Amendment by claiming "nobody" actually analyzed the information. Our government leaders evade the laws they are sworn to uphold by building prisons offshore where foreign nationals are illegally detained and tortured by "civilian" contractors. Officials appointed to direct the nation's Security Agencies lie to Congress regarding their activities. We are constantly at war. The war on drugs. The war on terror. We're constantly at war because in war, you can justify anything. Extreme circumstances, they tell us, require extreme measures.

How many times have we heard that throughout history? And when did it end well? Have we forgotten Nuremberg? America's true strength lies in her adherence to principles, not her military strength. If we forsake our principles in times of testing and trial, then we have already lost what is best in ourselves and our country.

Our fears are turning us into a nation of sheep. At the airport, we present our papers and stand in a scanner with no belt on our trousers, our bare feet planted on two yellow foot pads, and our hands over our heads while armed customs officials x-ray our baggage. Cameras peer down on us everywhere we go. We say that being watched doesn't affect us while we post filtered images of ourselves on social media or engage in virtue signaling rather than express our honest opinions.

Through it all, political pundits from the left and right come and go, each with their pet theory on how to fix the system. "If we change this here or tweak that there," a real-life version of War Machine with Russel Crowe succeeding Brad Pit.[107] No one ever stops to ask if maybe the system is the problem. Maybe people ultimately aren't supposed to be governed by systems; perhaps the Constitution was designed to protect us from them. Perhaps we are supposed to govern ourselves.

Learning to exercise freedom is like riding a bike: you'll never learn to ride until Dad lets go of the seat. Yes, you may fall, scrape your knee, or bang into a tree. Life is messy like that. But overcoming fear is the price you pay to become an adult. Outward compliance and inward conviction are not the same thing and do not produce the same results: one takes, the other gives. Compliance stems from coercion. Conviction flows from choice. Freedom must be defended because without it we can never reach our full potential as individuals and, ultimately, as a nation.

They claim our data belongs to them. That's nonsense. It is data about us, so it belongs to us. If we are going to protect our liberty, we must start with our privacy. They can't be separated. How do you vote? In private. There is a very good reason for that.

We must send our government a strong message that our rights are not for sale and that we will not suffer them to

---

[107] War Machine (2017)

be infringed upon, no matter what justification they are selling. Edward Snowden was right about that:

"And ultimately, the truth sinks in that no matter what justification you're selling yourself, this is not about terrorism. Terrorism is the excuse. This is about economic and social control."[108]

The intelligence community pays to build new technologies for social media platforms that collect and model data about us because they don't want to get their hands dirty. The government doesn't intervene because the *National Security–Information Technology Complex* is a symbiotic relationship in which the government relies on high-tech for intelligence and tax revenue, and tech companies rely on the government for R&D and contracts. As Eisenhower feared, the guardrails that separated the government and the private sector before WWII have all but vanished.

America's growing secularism is also contributing to the problem. The Declaration of Independence asserts that rights originate with God. If God is removed, where do rights come from? Rights that originate with the state are not rights. They are policies, and policies are subject to change.

These are lessons that take a lifetime to learn. When you are young and idealistic you believe in systems, but as you gain experience you realize there are no systems. There are just people: good and evil, and everything in between.

Privacy is more than our right; it is our divine heritage, and "to secure these rights, Governments are instituted among Men."

Finally, if we are to lay claim to these rights, we must be willing to extend them to others:[109]

---

[108] Snowden (2016)

[109] "What constitutes the bulwark of our own liberty and independence? It is not our frowning battlements, our bristling sea coasts, the guns...or the strength of

"You have the right to a fair trial. You have the right not to be detained without due process. You have the right not to be tortured."

We must never descend to the level of our enemies, lest we become the very thing we fight against. We must struggle for our ideals, not just to survive. That's what inspires Americans. It's what makes us great. No one can foretell the future because you never have all the information. That's why being principled is so critical. History has demonstrated time and time again what happens to individuals and nations that abandon their principles. Being smart means doing right, even when you can't see how things will work out.

Surveying the carnage resulting from the world's last near-fatal struggle against totalitarianism, MacArthur reflected:

As I look back on the long, tortuous trail from those grim days…when an entire world lived in fear, when democracy was on the defensive everywhere, when modern civilization trembled in the balance, I thank a merciful God that he has given us the faith, the courage and the power from which to mold victory. We have known the bitterness of defeat and the exultation of triumph, and from both we have learned there can be no turning back. We must go forward to preserve in peace what we won in war.

A new era is upon us…The destructiveness of the war potential, through progressive advances in scientific discovery, has in fact now reached a point which revises the traditional concepts of war.

Men since the beginning of time have sought peace..Military alliances, balances of power, leagues of nations, all in turn

---

failed, leaving the only path to be by way of the crucible of war. We have had our last chance. If we do not now devise some greater and more equitable system, Armageddon will be at our door. The problem basically is theological and involves a spiritual recrudescence and improvement of human character that will synchronize with our almost matchless advances in science, art, literature and all material and cultural developments of the past two thousand years, it must be of the spirit if we are to save the flesh."

The military created your phone, and that matters. Its technologies do not need to be altered to surveil or exert control. They were built for that; it is in their DNA. No one would disagree that we need technology and intelligence services to defend our country against all enemies, but we must never allow these capabilities to be turned against us, and we are coming perilously close to that.

Epilogue

As this book neared publication, the first feedback regarding opinions expressed within its pages began trickling in. I kept a mental list of critics' comments and quickly realized they fell into three distinct categories:

First, that the bleeding-edge technologies I discussed in the book's final sections, CBDCs and digital IDs, will never be implemented. To these critics I would say: how did you react when cryptocurrencies were introduced? Did you buy Bitcoin when it was selling for pennies—before they did away with pennies, that is? In most cases, this riposte is sufficient. However, since you bought this book, most probably to be entertained, but perhaps in hopes of learning something new, I would argue that CBDCs and digital IDs have already transcended the theoretical. Both have been under development for years, with many millions expended. All that is required now is the opportune moment.

Second, for those who trust government to safeguard their freedoms, I recommend studying historical instances where populations had their property confiscated. Without property, you are a stateless person, and stateless persons have few rights under the law. If you doubt this, visit any native reserve, or study the history of the Jews over the past two millennia, the Nazi treatment of displaced peoples during World War II, Pol Pot's agrarian reforms in Cambodia, the Palestinian camps on the West Bank, Stalin's treatment of the Kulaks in Ukraine, and so on.[110]

Third, to those who believe that our government would never get away with it, I would point out that

---

[110] Historically, the concept of terra nullius was used to justify the colonization of lands that were perceived as being uninhabited or uncultivated, even if they were inhabited by indigenous peoples. In effect, use it - which in most cases means map it, put a fence around it - or lose it.

lawmakers routinely perceive themselves as above the law. For example: in 1968, during the bloodiest days of the Vietnam War, officials from Nixon's campaign urged President Nguyễn Văn Thiệu's government to reject President Johnson's proposed peace plan, promising that Nixon would negotiate a better deal if elected. Johnson discovered the scheme because his office had bugged the South Vietnamese embassy in Washington. Although Johnson confronted Nixon and taped his denial, he could not publicly accuse Nixon without revealing his source, because bugging embassies is illegal.

Four years later, Nixon's operatives (one ex-CIA, the other ex-FBI) were apprehended breaking into the Democratic National Committee headquarters at the Watergate Complex to wiretap phones and steal documents. Nixon was forced to leave office but never charged. Clearly, only underlings need worry about jail time.

We lost control of our government the moment we consented to financing deficit spending through borrowing. You have to pay your taxes, or you will be incarcerated, but lenders can demand terms. In our current situation, where government debt runs into the tens of trillions, who are they more beholden to: taxpayers or lenders? The way to control government is by controlling its access to revenue.[111] Without money, governments are powerless.

Ironically, it was President Nixon who signed the Bank Secrecy Act into law, requiring the reporting of all private transactions over $10,000 to the government. While $10,000 was substantial in 1970, it's a mere pittance today due to inflation. Yet the government has never raised the limit or repealed the law. Why should the government care

---

[111] A lesson that Parliament brought to a head under Charles I of England in 1649.

what I do with my property? Where do they get *their right* to know?

Nine years later, the Third-Party Doctrine became law. The Third-Party Doctrine is a legal principle stating that individuals have a reduced expectation of privacy for information voluntarily shared with third parties, such as phone companies or banks. Law enforcement may access such information without a warrant, as it is not considered protected under the Fourth Amendment. When was the last time you "voluntarily" shared what you were doing on your phone or what you were purchasing with the government? Nod your head and click accept.

Finally, consider this: seatbelts were optional when I was a child. By the time I became a young man, they were mandatory, and non-compliance became an offense punishable by a fine.[112] Later, automobile manufacturers introduced a chime[113] to remind drivers to buckle up. Now, it continues ringing until you do. How long will it be before you are unable to start the engine until your seatbelt is fastened? This is how easily rights can be forfeited, how technology can be extended from prompting to enforcement - gradually, almost imperceptibly.

The implementation of CBDCs and Digital IDs, pregnant with the grave threat they pose to our rights and freedoms, is not only possible but, given the trajectory of technological development traced in this book, increasingly likely. All that remains to complete our transition from citizens to the disenfranchised is to nod our heads one last time and click "accept."

---

[112] Unless you live in New Hampshire.
[113] I would be remiss here if I did not point the reader to Pavlov's conditioning experiments.